Revelation
A thought for each day of the year

Philip M. Hudson

Copyright 2020 by Philip M. Hudson.

Published 2020.

Printed in the United States of America.

All rights reserved.

No portion of this book may be reproduced, stored in a retrieval system, or transmitted in any form or by any means - electronic, mechanical, photocopy, recording, scanning, or other - except for brief quotations in critical reviews or articles, without the prior written permission of the author.

ISBN 978-1-950647-35-4

Illustrations - Google Images.

This book may be ordered from online bookstores.

Publishing Services by BookCrafters
Parker, Colorado.
www.bookcrafters.net

Table of Contents

Acknowledgements...i
Preface..v
Introduction..vii

A Thought For Each Day Of The Year...1
About The Author...367
By The Author...369
What More Can I Say?..373

If we hope to follow the
divine design of God during the
complicated construction of our mortal
tabernacles, we must give our attention to
His counsel. We can only do so if we have the
faith to believe all that He has revealed, and all
that He now reveals. If, in the end, the eyes of our
understanding are opened to believe that He will yet
reveal many great and important things that relate
to our progression, we will be up and about on a
journey that leads to the successful completion
of our proper and perfect frames. We will be
blessed to retain certificates of occupancy,
so that we might invite the Spirit to
dwell with us.

Acknowledgements

In this volume, I have attributed quotations to original authors whenever possible, as well as when I have editorialized their ideas. In many cases, however, my language will naturally reflect the teachings of leaders and members of The Church of Jesus Christ of Latter-day Saints.

The list of those who have contributed to this book is endless. As I have organized my own thoughts, I have realized how heavily I have borrowed from the towering examples of those who, over the years, have been my mystical mentors, my sensible chaperones, my spiritual guides, my surrogate saviors, my compassionate critics, and everything in between.

They are my avatars, manifestations of deity in bodily forms, my na'vi, the visionaries, who communicate with God on a level to which I can only aspire, and my tsaddik, whom I esteem as intuitive interpreters of biblical law and scripture. They are my divine teachers incarnate. They have offered listening ears, extended open arms. lifted my spirits, shown me the way, stretched my mind, reinforced my faith, strengthened my testimony, helped me to discover my wings, given immaterial support, provided of their means, emboldened me with words of encouragement, cheered me on with wise counsel, taught me humility, been there to steady me, soothed my troubled soul, stepped in to nurture me, led me to fountains of living water, wet my parched lips with inspired counsel, and bound up my wounds.

When I think of the influence of a multitude of angels thinly disguised as my family, friends, and peers, I remember the words of Sir Isaac Newton, who, when pressed to reveal the great secret behind his accomplishments, simply replied: "I stood on the shoulders of giants." Of course, at the end of the day, I alone am responsible for the content of this volume. But I hope my interpretations of principles and doctrine will cultivate your interest to dig deeper into the themes woven into this tapestry, by turning to the scriptures and seeking inspiration from the Spirit. My only goal is to help you to expand your insights into the telestial mile markers, the terrestrial truths, and the celestial guidelines that accompany each of us during our quest for enlightenment through revelation.

Paul knew what it meant to go the second mile. He labored among the Corinthian Saints, whom he was pleased to discover had a working relationship with the laws and ordinances of the Gospel. He characterized the revelatory gifts of God as being written upon "tables of stone." That is well and good, but he hinted that there exists another order of mind. It is a connection that can be ours if we will embrace the ordinances of the Gospel: "Ye are manifestly declared to be the epistle of Christ ministered by us, written not with ink, but with the Spirit of the living God; not in tables of stone, but in fleshy tables of the heart." (2 Corinthians 3:3).

The Mountain
of the Lord's House
that is visualized in
scripture is an allegorical
and figurative description of
the refuge of Zion in the Last
Days, when it "shall be established
in the tops of the mountains." (2 Nephi
12:2). Whether it is a high place of God,
a place of revelation, or perhaps the temple
itself, Latter-day Saints are prone to restrict
the application of this phrase to one area, that
that of the intermountain west, specifically to
the valleys near the Great Salt Lake. But this
interpretation may be too narrow. When we
feel the influence of the Spirit, we are
drawn to believe it to be the invisible
summit of our imagination, where
cool air exists, and where the
one true and living God
dwells.

Preface

I love to learn by reading the scriptures, and I often think of St. Hilary, who wrote in the third century: "Scripture consists not in what we read, but in what we understand." In each of the musings within this volume, I have consistently tried to find a scriptural foundation and a spiritual confirmation as I put my pen to paper.

I am continually reminded of Nephi's counsel to press forward with complete dedication and steadfastness, or confidence with a firm determination in Christ, having a perfect brightness of hope, or perfect faith, and charity, or a love of God and of all men. If we do this, feasting upon the word of Christ, or receiving strength and nourishment as we ponder the doctrines of the kingdom, and particularly the phenomenon of revelation, and as we then endure to the end in righteousness, we shall have eternal life, which is the greatest of God's gifts. (See 2 Nephi 31:20).

It is with love, then, that I extend to you the invitation to enjoy this omnibus of random thoughts. Embrace it at face value, and use its observations relating to baptism as a springboard to your own personal plateaus of discovery, as you are taught by the Spirit to move in the direction of your dreams.

We partake of the emblems of the Sacrament that we might overcome our spiritual death by coming into the presence of our Father and His Son, by way of the Holy Ghost. His Spirit dazzles us with an endless reserve of revelation. It provides illumination to every corner of our minds and our spirits. The promised blessings that are proffered by the combined capacity of the intrinsic light that radiates from all three members of the Godhead is virtually beyond description. The binding covenant that is articulated in the prayer bridges the gulf between the secular and the divine that, in other circumstances, might exist for us. It is no small coincidence that the names of the Father, the Son, and the Holy Ghost are referenced by name in the words of the prayer.

Introduction

If they are fortunate, novice quilters quickly learn a bit of wisdom from the Amish, who make some of the finest quilts in the world. On purpose, the Amish build mistakes into their projects, because they believe that any attempt on their part to design and produce a flawless creation would be a mockery of God, Who alone is perfect. The humility of the Amish makes me think of my own weak attempts to put the thoughts expressed in this omnibus to paper. In His infinite wisdom, God knows very well that I do not need to consciously plan on lacing my efforts with errors. That will come quite naturally, without the need for me to intentionally contribute to my short-comings.

Perhaps this serendipitous collection of musings will do little more than help to define quirks in my personality. Each of us is different, and many things, including our family and friends, the circumstances in which we find ourselves, the quality of our education, and our own personalities, inspire and mold our oral and written expressions. I would like to think that, in this text, all of these influences have been encouraging, affirmative, and constructive.

The reflections within this tome leave the door ajar for the reader, to allow shafts of the light of understanding to creep in. If, as I have expressed my thoughts, I mis-stated myself a few times, or flat-out got it wrong, I ask the patient indulgence and gentle correction of the reader.

Too often, I realize that my communications can be "carefully disguised with hypocrisy and glittering words," as Einstein put it. Although I do fancy myself a wordsmith, I have tried to avoid pedestrian expressions, idle language, and lazy scholarship. I do not pretend to be an authority on revelation, inasmuch as I believe that we are all works in progress, but if you find the factual tone of a particular musing disengaging, the truth is that I typically experienced a deep personal involvement in my interpretation of the principles that illuminated its meaning.

In any event, when you open this volume, I hope you ponder these minute musings with as much enjoyment as I have experienced while creating them.

In the Church,
we sometimes will have a
striking experience when light
and truth distil upon our souls.
Just so, in the Sacred Grove, light
"descended gradually," entering the
quiet grove slowly enough that Joseph
was able to gauge its approach until it
finally reached him and enveloped him
within a dazzling brilliance. It was only
then that he "saw two Personages, whose
brightness and glory (were beyond all)
description," and who stood suspended
in the air within the encircling light.
(J.S.H. 1:17). We may not see Them,
but when we are in the presence
of those from the unseen world,
we receive inspiration and
revelation, and we can be
sure that we are in
holy precincts.

As long as we remain in a state of rebellion against the Spirit, the fruit of the Tree of Life must remain just beyond our reach, even if, for the sake of curiosity, we now and then would like to take a bite. If we never raise our eyes to search eternal horizons, the world before us will appear as nothing more than a barren desert that is devoid of refreshing oases, the welcome shade of trees, and an abundance of well watered gardens. If we lack faith to nourish revelation thru the Spirit, not even its living water will be able to sustain us.

Revelation that comes from God speaks a language that is universally understood without ambiguity. It leaves little room for discussion as to its meaning because it is spiritually discerned. Even more remarkable, it unifies us even as it recognizes our diversity. It quickly moves us away from dependence and independence, to interdependence. However, it blesses us with unity and conformity without asking us to give up our individuality, or those things that make us unique. It invites us to come unto God and to "partake of his goodness; (and it reminds us that) he denieth none that come unto him, black and white, bond and free, male and female; and he remembereth the heathen; and all are alike unto God, both Jew and Gentile."
(2 Nephi 26:33).

All around us,
we see the fulfillment
of the prophecy that we are
living in the Last Days, when the
hearts of men shall fail them, as
their shields of faith begin to falter.
When the heavens close, the revelatory
voice of warning is silenced, and all is
quiet from pulpits that were once aflame
with faith. The rebellious rant and rave
against that which is good, but we can
also be pacified, and lulled away into
a false sense of carnal security, until
we believe that all is well in Zion. But
none of us can afford to take our
foot off the gas pedal during our
journey along the highway that
leads to heaven's gate.

If we do as the Lord has commanded, our comprehension of the emblems of the Sacrament will flow easily and poetically to our minds. Our persistence and our participation will lead to practiced fluency with the language of the Spirit that is the result of the inspiration that will come as we approach the ordinance with faith, fasting, and prayer. As our minds are enlightened, we will be cast off into a stream of revelation and swept up in the quickening currents direct experience with our Heavenly Father, with His Son Jesus Christ, and with the Holy Ghost.

If we hope to follow the
divine design of God during the
complicated construction of our mortal
tabernacles, we must give our attention to
His counsel. We can only do so if we have the
faith to believe all that He has revealed, and all
that He now reveals. If, in the end, the eyes of our
understanding are opened to believe that He will yet
reveal many great and important things that relate
to our progression, we will be up and about on a
journey that leads to the successful completion
of our proper and perfect frames. We will be
blessed to obtain certificates of occupancy,
so that we might invite the Spirit to
dwell with us.

As we begin to embrace the
creative expression of revelation,
we recognize how its energy can help
us to comprehend God. We feel the divine
potential within us. We feel the confidence
to ask seemingly innocent questions that will
have profound answers and implications that
shake our world and spread like the ripples
radiating outward from a rock thrown into
the still water of a pond. We begin to see
the answers to our humble inquiries as
a revelatory machine for the
making of Gods.

Revelation
unshackles us
from the unpleasant
consequences of Justice.
Darkness is the conjoined twin
of misery, but the obedience of faith
frees us to embrace the truth, to make
intelligent choices, to perform purposefully,
to carry on convincingly, and to persistently
progress; to dismiss the cares of the world through
the Atonement of Jesus Christ; to ascend into the
rarified atmosphere of the Spirit that invites us
to inhale deeply; that we might be powerfully
reinvigorated by refreshing communication
from our Heavenly Father.

As we open our hearts to the revealed word of the Lord, it will be as it was in the days of King Josiah, when he "went up into the house of the Lord, and all the men of Judah and all the inhabitants of Jerusalem with him, and the priests, and the prophets, and all the people, both small and great. And (they) made a covenant before the Lord, to walk after the Lord, and to keep his commandments and his testimonies and his statutes with all their heart and all their soul, (and) to perform the words of the covenant. And all the people stood to the covenant." (2 Kings 23:2-3).

Revelation from God
sets us free to be creative,
and our creativity sets us free to
properly plan before we come face to
face with the crises of life. It prevents
our poor performance and it mitigates
consequences. As we learn to rely upon
the doctrine of Christ that is taught by
the Spirit, we internalize its elements.
This allows us to surrender ourselves
to its infinite possibilities, without
reservation. Therein, we find our
individuality and avenues for
personal expression, and in
the end, we discover our
freedom to "become."

After the dust
settles, when Church
leaders have been quoted
and all the scriptures have been
cited, the fact remains that we have
not received the revelations that answer
the questions that relate to our progression
between kingdoms of glory. But intuitively,
we want to believe that it is possible. When
we attend the temple as patrons, and we
perform vicarious work for the dead,
when the veil is almost transparent,
and we sense inaudible whispering
from the other side, the Spirit
speaks to us in a language
of peace regarding the
absolute perfection
of God's Plan of
Happiness.

If we thoughtlessly postpone our quest for the holy grail of revelation until we have become spiritually blinded to the Light of Christ, we become subject to the spirit of the devil. When he captures our hearts, they are mutated to become stony and cold, and we lose the capacity to distinguish good from evil and light from darkness. When we exchange the sunshine that is generated by the whisperings of the Spirit for the wintry weather of worldliness, it will withdraw and move on to warmer climes, allowing Satan's icy breath to be sucked into the vortex we have created for him.

Without
knowledge,
there can be no
faith; without faith,
there can be no light,
and without the light of
revelation from the heavens
there can be no recognition
of religious truth; and without
spiritual enlightenment, if just
one of these three elements is
missing, all must be forsaken.
Our fortunes rest on the basis
of how completely we have
embraced our intuitions,
our inspiration, and
revelation itself.

As our
testimonies of
Christ swell in our
hearts, it is faith that
intensifies our yearning to
receive revelation from God.
The Gospel centers our lives, to
bring them into harmony with true
principles. We strive to be obedient,
so that we might find ourselves in a
constant state of improvement. As we
begin to believe in ourselves, we find
it is that much easier to believe our
Father in Heaven, too. It is with a
quickening pulse that we realize
that our progress is headed in
the direction of perfection.
God is perfect; He does
not make knock-offs.
We are the right
stuff.

We are at a crossroads, for our decision to believe in revelation from God will deify us, just as our choice not to believe can destroy us. How we respond to the mighty lightning, thunder, and burning bush of Sinai that summons us to come unto the Savior of the world will delineate our dreams and will define our destiny. Ultimately, it will determine how, where, and with whom we will spend all of eternity.

Whenever
Latter-day Saints
cannot find resources
within the Church to sustain
their connection to Deity that
had been established by revelation,
they are at risk of sliding back into
marginalized relationships that may even
brand them as "less active," or "inactive."
Fundamentally, they lose direction, power,
and purpose, because they have lost the
means to nourish, support, and sustain
interpersonal connections that are
driven by revelatory principles
that had, at one time, been
their guiding lights.

Revelation from God leaves a distinct afterglow from our pre-mortal lives and establishes an undeniable link between the heavens and the earth. A simple yet uncommitted recognition of Jesus will not qualify us to inherit the Celestial Kingdom. Christians of convenience lack the revelatory fire that is ignited by faith. Many honorable people who accept the Savior will still inherit the Terrestrial Kingdom. According to the scriptures, these are they who "received not the Gospel, neither the testimony of Jesus, neither the prophets, neither the everlasting covenant. Last of all, these are all they who will not be gathered with the Saints, to be caught up unto the Church of the Firstborn, and received into the cloud." (D&C 76:101-102).

The effects of sin are inevitable and inescapable, but for the intercession by faith of the Atonement. The Maker and Fashioner of the universe must intervene in our behalf by implementing His Plan to engage laws that are designed to restore equilibrium. Only if we believe in revelation, can we begin to understand that "in the heavens, there is a "better and an enduring substance." (Hebrews 10:34). It is heavenly guidance that makes it possible for us to handle and mold that substance into the elixir of the gods.

A number of the chapters in the story of our lives have already been set to type, and we don't know how many remain to be written. But this we know: The fairytale was created by Heavenly Father, and we must honor its premise that we are His sons and daughters. We cannot start over and make a new beginning, but we can begin now, and with the help of a talented and gifted Ghostwriter Whose real name is the Holy Ghost, write a brand new revelatory ending to the chapters that are our contributions to The Plan of God.

Sometimes all too quickly, and at other times agonizingly slowly, those who have sold their souls to the Devil for a mess of pottage are dragged down to a hell on earth that is of their own construction. Their bad habits are the result of repetitively impulsive behaviors that, in a rising tide of wickedness, continually erode away at the foundations of agency. They are fettered by the chains of compulsions. They realize too late that unlimited freedom leads to tyranny. The Holy Ghost has the power, however, to lead them back to the path of safety through the Atonement, by way of revelation from God and the perfect law of liberty.

The cataracts that are created by our concessions to sin cloud our vision. Our narrow perspective forces us into making comfortless compromises, leaving the landscapes of our lives as nothing more than empty shells. If we do not take advantage of the therapy that is offered by the Holy Ghost, and gratefully receive the revelation of God, our prognosis must remain poor. He is a heavenly optometrist for eyes that have lost the ability to see clearly, and that can no longer make the distinctions between good and evil and between light and darkness, and even between pleasure and pain. He can restore our vision to 20:20.

Without
the spiritual and
priesthood power that is
received by revelation we must
remain ever learning, while never
coming to a knowledge of the truth
that would make us free. We grasp at
straws, failing to recognize that nothing
will kill our creativity more quickly than
the self-assurance that poisons our ability
to recognize the revelatory influence
of awesome powers that are greater
than ourselves, that literally
defy description.

As we study the
elements of The Plan
of Salvation, it seems that
our faith should remain fixed
on the revelations the Lord has
given us that relate to our world,
and not on mysteries that have not
been revealed to us, may never be
revealed, or that just may not
be pertinent to our current
circumstances.

Revelation may be recognized only when we have allowed ourselves to fall under the influence of the Spirit. That will happen only if we are in a state of harmony with The Plan. Our acceptance of communication from the heavens waits upon our initiative. It is not subject to amendment, to our private interpretation, or to the scrutiny of faithless sceptics.

The Spirit
teaches that
darkness cannot
abide the illumination
of faith. We will seize the
opportunity to be enveloped
in light, as we learn to face
the sunshine of revelation that
is of God. If shadows still exist,
they will always remain behind
us. The traveling companions of
gloom that take the form of
apprehension and timidity
will remain out of sight,
and out of mind, and
powerless to exert
their murky
hold on
us.

Those who are
ignorant among us are
forever attempting to drag
communication from the heavens
down to their own level so that it is
in harmony with their myopic view of
life. The world ridicules revelation and
disparages its delivery, and scorns even
the most basic elements of The Plan.
But such feeble efforts must surely
ring hollow when compared to
the thunder, lightning, and
burning bush that was
never consumed
on Sinai.

One of the articles of
faith of The Church of Jesus
Christ of Latter-day Saints is that
its members believe that The Plan of
God provides us with institutional and
personal continuing revelation that comes
from Heavenly Father through the medium
of the Holy Ghost. If we are "looking for
the spectacular," we might just miss out
on "the constant flow of revealed
communication that comes."
(Spencer W. Kimball).

Whenever the white-hot
spark of revelation has been struck
off the Divine Anvil of God, it ignites an
incendiary flame whose shimmering trail can
be traced across the sky, all the way back to
heaven. If we yield to the natural inclination
to suppress revelation by dousing it with the
water of worldliness, if we try to contain
it within the fire line of faithlessness,
or if we bury it under the sand of
skepticism, and especially if we
throw the dirt of doubt on it,
we will never be blessed to
know His mind or will.
(See Alma 19:6)

We know that
God is sensitive to our
needs, because we have the
evidence of our effectual and
fervent prayers. For as long as we
are in conformity to the laws of
heaven that govern The Plan of
Salvation, we draw virtue from
its life force. We figuratively
reach out and touch the hem
of the garment of Jesus
Christ, to feel the spirit
of revelation, even if
it seems that we are
within the press of
the crowd.

The
Holy Ghost
is our mentor and
our teacher. If we are
good students, and have
done our homework, He will
reward us with an illumination
of the principles of The Plan that
will bathe our minds in a cascade
of insight, intuition, inspiration,
and revelation. He will give us
the answer key to the exam
we will take following
the conclusion of our
curriculum in
mortality.

As
we endure
in faith, precious
emanations of familiar
and soothing oscillations
of energy will resonate from
within the limitless reserves of the
Spirit. These are selflessly shared by
the One who has promised to carry us
along on rolling waves of revelation
toward a shoreline of stability that
nurtures a more sure witness of
the Savior's divinity, no matter
what the tide may bring
in tomorrow.

Our careful and prayerful study of scripture helps us to obtain an eternal perspective. Jacob revealed the formula. He said "We search the prophets, and we have many revelations and the spirit of prophecy; and having all these witnesses we obtain a hope, and our faith (in Christ is) unshaken." (Jacob 4:6).

Revelation
is as a mortar
that binds together
the building blocks of
our testimonies. It is the
footing of our conversion.
The foundation cornerstones
of the Gospel of Jesus Christ
are continually bathed and
washed clean and pure in
its living water.

We,
who have
the faith to
be born again,
are set free by the
perfect Law of Liberty
to reach our potential.
We are as the acorns of
mighty oaks, vitalized by
the revelation of the word
of God to bask within His
encouraging influence, to
grow to the full stature
of our spirits.

Without
the guidance
of the Holy Spirit,
Whose influence is
revelatory in its very
nature, we risk becoming
more comfortable with our
own perceptions of truth than
we are with His omniscience. We
pit our own marginal capabilities
against God's priesthood power,
our own paltry overtures against
His almighty works, and our
stubborn won't against
His gentle will.

It is only thru the phenomenon of the continuing, enduring, immeasurable, infinite, uncorrupted, unfathomable, uninterrupted, and unspoiled grace that is embodied within revelation from above, that we find ourselves "swallowed up in the joy of ... God, even to the exhausting of (our) strength." (Alma 27:17).

We are
exposed to a
constant stream of
insight and intuition,
as well as of inspiration
and revelation, that flows
from above in a cascade of
creativity. A divine direction
dictates that we walk along
illuminated pathways as we
implement our faculties of
mind and spirit, in order
to understand The Plan
that God has in mind
for each one of us.

Wo unto those who groan under darkness and under the bondage of sin. They squander precious resources groping about in a frantic but fruitless search for meaning in their lives. In short, they fail to appreciate the stabilizing power that could have been theirs if they had only focused upon the nurturing influence of revelation from God.

Sooner or later,
there is for each of
us who has undergone a
spiritual heart transplant a
moment in the sun, when the
steady light of understanding
illuminates our minds with the
revelation of the Word of God.
He confirms our divine potential
by quickening our new organs,
and by initiating an unbroken
sinus rhythm that establishes
a perfect harmony with
the heavens.

During our worship, there may come a time when we "see the light." We may be dazzled by an A-ha! moment, when we have an instant of sudden insight, intuition, inspiration, and even revelation, which is made known to all the children of God by the obedience of faith.

The Lord is sensitive to our needs and He teaches us how to pray to the Father both effectually and fervently. When we are in conformity to the laws of the Gospel, virtue will flow from a life force that is the Spirit of heaven. We figuratively reach out, that we might touch the hem of the Savior's garment, to bask within His revelatory influence, even if we remain in the press of the crowd.

In between
the sights and
sounds, rides and
attractions, and thrills
and spills of our earthly
theme-park experience, it is
revelation that teaches us to
use spiritual hygiene practices
to remove the grit and grime
that accumulates as a part of
life, but that always threaten
to foul our inner workings
and curtail our sensitivity
to the impressions that
come to each of us
from heaven.

It is within
the structure of
the principles, and
the doctrines, and the
ordinances of the temple
that our experiences in the
learning laboratories of life
begin to make sense. Therein
lies the inherent beauty of The
Plan and the key to its success.
Our revelatory experiences will
teach that "the brotherhood of
man is an integral element of
Christianity no less than is the
Fatherhood of God, and to
deny one is no less infidel
than to deny the other."
(Lyman Abbott).

As in a heavenly tongue that is at the same time melodious, rhythmical, and soothing to our ears, it is calming to our souls when we hear the Spirit whisper: "You're a stranger here." We are quickly comforted by the realization that we have "wandered from a more exalted sphere." That road from glory, and our pathway back to God's Celestial Kingdom, are illuminated by revelation. Our discipleship is actively linked to our faith that the heavens are not closed; that our Father continues to speak to us. (Eliza R. Snow).

The faithful find mentors whom they can emulate, instead of scapegoats that are easy to blame. Instead of looking for easier answers, they dig deeply in the revelations to uncover healthier solutions to the problems they face.

We
never thirst
when we are
anchored through
Gospel topsoil into
the source of living
water, due to our total
reliance upon the Spirit.
Revelation might be the
definitive expression of
honesty with ourselves,
with Heavenly Father,
with the Savior, and
with the Holy
Ghost.

Faith becomes a celestial bridge that transports the righteous past the vicissitudes of life all the way to the steadiness of the kingdom of God that is found in revelation and lies above the confusion of turmoil.

Faith
carries us
to the edge
of eternity, to
the very portals
of heaven, where
"forever" stands
revealed in a
mind bending
panorama
that lies
before
us.

The faithful know how to turn stumbling blocks into stepping stones. Crisis becomes opportunity, and victory is snatched from the jaws of defeat. They know that revelation can come "like a flash of lightning and a clap of thunder. The people may shrink in fear, but after the storm, flowers will bloom."
("I Ching").

The faithful see their revelatory rapture as an "enchanted wood where the foliage is always green, where joy abides, and where nightingales nest and sing, and where life and death are one in the presence of the Lord Jesus." (Helen Keller).

Our
faith is that
there is enough
room and enough
time in the eternities
for each of us develop
the ability to see beyond
the limited horizon of our
vision all the way to the
heavens by the power of
the revelations of God.
The Atonement of Jesus
Christ becomes as our
golden ticket that
guarantees our
safe passage
home.

Some
recognize
the anchor of
faith as intuition,
or as the capacity to
understand something
without the need for our
conscious reasoning. It is
in good company, for it
draws upon insight, and
is the precursor of not
only inspiration, but
also of revelation,
that can be as a
thunder from
heaven.

We seek
revelations
of God, because
we do not want to
be spiritually starved,
doctrinally dehydrated,
or intellectually inhibited
while only inches away from
the living bread that could
have satisfied our hunger,
or from the fountains of
living water that could
have slaked our thirst
or even healed us of
our sins and our
blemishes.

In the world, there is an ever-present negative energy that influences us, and the promptings that come to us from the Holy Ghost in the form of revelations that drive us to our knees, are its only possible countermeasures. The only stipulations are that we confess when we have, in any magnitude, embraced the opposites that lie before us, and that we immediately undertake the safety protocols required by repentance to bring us back to harmony with heaven.

Revelation
detoxifies us
from the cares
of the world and
homogenization of
our standards, even
as we are subjected to
the vicissitudes of life.
It allows us to return to
the hallowed halls of the
Spirit, to be re-vitalized as
we are re-introduced to
God's magical kingdom
where dreams really
do come true.

Experience
is the active
ingredient in a
fertile matrix that
was carefully created
by our Father in Heaven
during His preparation of
the petri dish that has been
personalized to match our
individual circumstances,
in the exciting learning
laboratory of life. But
He doesn't expect us
to conduct these
experiments
alone.

By venturing forth out of our comfort zones and inviting the Spirit to guide us, we enlarge the foundation of our spiritual center and we make room for faith. If we will embrace our divine center that lies in the spirit of revelation, we will follow a yellow brick road with our hearts, might, minds, and strength until we finally reach the Emerald City of Oz.

Allowing the
spirit of revelation to
release us from captivity
through faith permits us to
see things as they really are,
and enjoy a lucidity that will
comes more from the heart than
the head. From the vantage point
of revelation, we can see things
more clearly. It is as if we have
escaped our mortal clay with its
confining limitations that can
distort our perspective and
twist our attention inward,
toward worldliness.

There is no
revelation where
there is no student,
and if we do not ask
the right questions that
relate to the Atonement
of Jesus Christ, we will be
at odds with our faith. We
will be doomed to receive
the wrong answers. Sadly,
rational minds will never
be able to bridge the gap
that must exist between
the profane character
of the worldly-wise
and our divine
nature.

At first, it may be the easier wrong that appears to be more convenient, but that is only because it harmonizes with the values of Babylon. Worldliness surrounds us, and without the stabilizing influence of the revealed word of God, our moral equivocation can far too easily become the easier way out, and become the pattern of our conduct.

When
we surrender
our hopes, our
aspirations, and
and our dreams to
a reality that denies
revelation, we will have
sold our birthright to the
lowest bidder for a mess of
pottage. Once we have made
the exchange, we may far too
easily be dragged down to hell
on earth, where we realize that
the prison into which we have
been unceremoniously cast is
of our own construction. If
there is no vision, if we
will not embrace the
revealed word of
God, we must
perish.

When we feel
the energy of faith
building within us, we
realize that it can lift us
to the zenith of experience,
until the lines distinguishing
mortality from eternity blur.
At that moment, when we find
ourselves in a condition that,
for the lack of better words,
can only be described as if
we were being born again,
we will be consumed in
a revelatory fire, or
in everlasting
burnings.

It is
the spirit
of revelation
that provides every
thread within the fabric
of our own faith a vitality,
vim, vigor, and vivacity that
is unique to holy vestments.
Their steadfast colors will
never fade, save it be thru
neglect or unbelief. They
will remain impervious
to blemishes, except
for the stain of
unresolved
sin.

We press
forward in the
light of the Spirit,
and with revelation
we are blessed with an
illumination of Gospel
principles that will bathe
our minds in a cascade of
inspiration and revelation.
We repent of our sins, and
renounce our fallen nature
that is nothing more than
a shadowy after-image
of the rebellion of
Lucifer at the
Council.

The light
of the body
is the eye, and
when it is single
to the faith to see
into heaven above,
our elements below
will be stirred by
its warm glow,
for we will be
captivated by
the spirit of
revelation.

It is by our faith to see all the way to heaven that the power of the Holy Ghost is released to penetrate the barriers that isolate us from the sum and substance of an existence that more accurately defines our reality.

The Holy Ghost, together with angels in heaven, holds His breath in hopeful anticipation while waiting upon our initiative to open our hearts to receive the revelatory word of God.

It is revelation that nurtures our dream that we might feel the gentle caress of the Master's hand, as our spiritual muscles are massaged by faith. We want Him to mold us and shape us as the Artisan of our destiny.

Disorder and progression must ultimately be in balance with each other. In fact, it was ordained in heaven that there must be a healthy juxtaposition of opposing forces for faith to prevail as the first principle in revealed religion, and for revelation to shortly fall on its heels.

We can be fully committed to The Plan of God and still have very special moments of reconfirmation. The Spirit sometimes works so powerfully upon us that we can say that our hearts have been changed through faith on the name of Christ, that we have been born of Him, and that we have become His Sons and daughters. We no longer have the disposition to do evil, but to do good continually.

The
insolvency of
the seduction that
has been perpetrated
by the Devil can only be
terminated by a third-party
bailout. The only solution to
his nepotism is for us to listen
to the revelatory promptings of
our One True Benefactor, Who is
none other than the Holy Ghost,
our Silent Partner, and our
Institutional Investor,
the third member of
the Godhead.

When we walk in
the light of life and
we go out of our way to
grasp the principles of truth,
we brim over with gratitude as
we explore our accommodations in
the household of faith, discovering that
they offer unobstructed views of the Holy
Ghost. We realize that when God unveiled
our world, and said: "Let there be light!" it
was a simple statement of fact as much as
it was a command. It was His invitation
to us to recognize, embrace, and to
celebrate the celestial energy that
is dancing all around us in a
revelatory rapture.

As we receive revelation, the Lord will go before our face, and will be on our right and and on our left; His Spirit will be in our hearts, and angels round about us to bear us up. (See D&C 84:88). How could we then think to turn away from such reinforcement, return to our wickedness, and determine to go it alone, without the guidance of the Holy Ghost?

Timid souls
who are cautiously
hesitant and tentatively
faithful don't consciously
intend to lose intimacy with
revelation. It can just fade
away, like a slow leak in an
automobile tire, and not as a
blowout. But, it may often be
traced back to the tendency
to mischief that may have
taken root during a time
period of particularly
intense vulnerability
to the wiles of
the Devil.

Because of our failure to recognize revelation from God, our society is in a self-destruct mode. D&C 1:16 cautions us that it seeks "not the Lord to establish his righteousness, but every man walketh in his own way, and after the image of his own god, whose image is in the likeness of the world, and whose substance is that of an idol, which waxeth old and shall perish in Babylon, even Babylon the great, which shall fall."

Standing in
opposition to the
Light of the Spirit is
a darkness that has the
potential to cover the earth,
and gross darkness the people.
Without the revelatory influence
of the Holy Ghost to intervene in
our behalf by introducing us to
the Atonement of Christ, we
would forever be subject
to the evil source of
that darkness, to
rise no more.

There will be
a day for each one of us
when we come face to face with
eternity and the spiritual element
in which we are then immersed will
transform our mortal clay. Until that
time arrives, while we yet tarry upon the
earth, we might ask ourselves under what
circumstances does that element quicken us,
and how can the pure knowledge that flows
out of it be vitalized? Surely, it is "a man's
wisdom (that will make) his face to shine,
(and) the boldness of his face shall be
changed." (Ecclesiastes 8:1). These
miracles occur as we embrace the
mighty winds of revelation that
flow from the Spirit of
the Lord.

Revelation from God teaches us that it is only those who passionately embrace the Gospel with its divine tutorial training who will go to the highest degrees of glory to live in the presence of the Gods. "These are they who are priests and kings, who have received of his fullness, and of his glory; and are priests of the Most High, after the order of Melchizedek, which was after the the order of Enoch, which was after the order of the Only Begotten Son. Wherefore, as it is written, they are (as the) gods, even the sons of God." (D&C 76:56-58).

Our worship on
the Sabbath day spawns
creativity. Our innovation can
be incremental or revolutionary,
but its end result is always revelatory.
The trickle-down economics of originality
during our Sabbath day services increases value.
The focus of our attention is not only on the end
point, but also on the process. We are invited to
enjoy the journey as much as we are prepared
to anticipate the destination. The paradox is
that all good things come only to those
who patiently wait upon the Lord.

If we do not rely
upon the light-generating
capacity of revelation, we are
doomed to dance about in flickering
shadows that illuminate nothing but the
caricatures of reality. The blind will stumble
about in the dark until the discrepancy between
their marginalized behavior and the ideals of
the Gospel of Jesus Christ becomes so great
that their short-lived pleasure in worldly
ways will evaporate as the morning
dew in the full light of day.

The
day is not
far off when our
mortal bodies must
put on immortality. This
may be accomplished as our
Heavenly Father carries us into
the greater dawn of heaven. Just as
ultraviolet light is used in sterilization,
(ultraviolet germicidal irradiation - UVGI),
could it be that it is the physical phenomenon
of the unearthly light that is intrinsic to God
that purifies and renews our sin-stained souls?
The revelatory power of God has something to
do with the change that will come over us,
when we become new creatures, and
all old things ae passed away.
(See 2 Corinthians 5:27).

Those of God's
children who have grown to
His spiritual stature will enjoy
His revelatory gifts to behold the
glory of the Celestial Kingdom, and in
particular "the transcendent beauty of the
gate through which the heirs of that kingdom
will enter, which (is) like unto circling flames
of fire; Also the blazing throne of God, wherein
(shall be) seated the Father and the Son." And
the "beautiful streets of that kingdom" will
appear to be paved with gold. (D&C 137:
2-4). This moving imagery describes
the power inherent in the spirit of
revelation, that can make our
lives sublime, as we leave
behind our footprints
on the sand of
time.

Thanks be to God for the
revelatory teaching that hell is a
reformatory that has been designed to
improve the quality of our moral nature. It
is a penitentiary where faith can still convict us
of our sins. It was designed to help disobedient
spirits recognize that Christ is the Mediator of the
Covenant through His infinite Atonement. In D&C
76, we learn that the Gospel was taught to those
kept in that prison. If, while there, they exercise
free will to accept not only Christ, but also the
fulness of His Gospel, is it within the realm of
possibility that they too might inherit celestial
glory with the Saints. This is why, in Sabbath
day services, we learn about temples, where
vicarious work is performed, not just
just a select few, but for all of
our kindred dead.

From the beginning
of time, Heavenly Father has
determined to keep open the lines of
communication between heaven and earth,
and to reveal His will to all of His children,
because, in a sense, each of us is confined to
a world our own making, and most of us are
trapped within the narrowly defined perceptual
prisons that we create for ourselves. Its walls
are reinforced by the razor-wire of limiting
beliefs, those stories we tell ourselves that
sabotage our own best efforts. Without the
revelatory power of our Father in Heaven,
they can damage or even cripple our
lives by diminishing our abilities,
compromising our progress, and
preventing us from reaching
our potential.

Revelation
nurtures harmony
with eternity. When our
eye is single to the glory
of God, we are liberated
from confinement to the
inexorable immutability
of the laws governing
our temporal world,
and we are out and
about, and busily
involved in our
Father's work
and glory.

It is
the revelation
that flows from the
bedrock of heaven that
transforms our timidity into
a powerful presence of mind.
Thereby, God creates a platform
for assertive action. On the other
hand, if we try to shirk the demands
that are put upon us by His word, we
will be swallowed up by a leviathan that
is no less tangible than that which was
experienced by Jonah, and we will
likewise eventually be spit out
upon the rocky shoreline
of our obligations.

Scribes and Pharisees who have little or no faith in the power of God to reveal His will, omit the weightier matters relating to His laws. They strain at gnats and swallow camels. Although they may appear to be righteous, inside they are "full of extortion and excess." (Matthew 23:25). Our righteous desire to choose to believe revealed truth with the wisdom of faith brings us closer to our Savior, the Lord Jesus Christ, leaving no room for hypocrisy to creep into our lives.

We follow the
yellow brick road
with our heart, might,
mind, and strength until
we have reached the Emerald
City of Oz. Our faith compels us
to trust in God's revealed will rather
than in the devilish doctrines that have
been concocted by the world's apologists.
God's buoyant messages invite us to believe
that our lives are wonderful "fairy tales
that are just waiting to be written" by
His omnipotent hand. (Hans
Christian Anderson).

Revelation
from Father
in Heaven points
us in the direction
of doctrine, so that
when we encounter the
principles of His Plan, we
will all experience religious
recognition, or a re-knowing
of things we have previously
been taught. We will respond
to the truth with actions that
have the form and substance
of a godly walk, and that
are bold testaments of
the power of His
word.

Revelation that comes
from God is a lynchpin that
waits for those moments in time
to figuratively tap us on the shoulder
and offer us opportunities to accomplish
great things that are unique to us and fitted
to our talents. It would be a tragedy of cosmic
proportion and eternal significance if we allowed
ourselves to remain unprepared or unqualified to
receive communication from the heavens that
could have defined our finest hour. (Sir
Winston Churchill, paraphrased).

When we open our hearts
to revelation from God, we
are consumed by His divine fire.
We are full of faith, as we engage
in our Father's business. Idleness, on
the other hand, is the workshop of the
Devil, and our refusal to embrace the
Plan is sin, for it wastes our precious
resources in futile pursuits, when we
should have been engaged in other
and more worthwhile activities for
which we would have been blessed
with wisdom and understanding.
Revelation would have flowed
unto us, and it would have
been wet with the dew
of heaven. (See
Daniel 4:15).

Disciples of Christ
whose spiritual welfare
depends upon a consistent
diet of continuing revelation,
would never think to consider
postponing their enrollment in
the curriculum patterned after
heaven, nor would they defer
their Gospel-oriented studies
in favor of worldly pursuits
that ask for pitifully little
in terms of commitment
or effort, and that
offer very little
in terms of
reward.

If mortality could be visualized in spatial dimensions, it would take the shape of an hourglass, with the strait gate represented by its narrow midsection. After passing through that constriction following a revelatory awakening by the Holy Ghost, we will experience the dawn of a new day, and amazing vistas will open up before our eyes, to reveal unparalleled opportunity.

Of ourselves, we lack the power to start over and make a new beginning, but with revelations, we can begin to create a new ending. With the help of our Savior, we can rewrite our life's story. In truth, they are fairytales that are simply waiting to be written by the finger of of God.

As long as
we have donned the
life vest of revelation,
and it remains securely in
place, we will be prepared to
deal with whatever challenges
the rapids of life might choose
to throw our way. High water
can even be our friend, as
it propels us down the
river of experience,
carrying us in the
direction of our
dreams.

We think
that we can be
happy if we wander
and play. But we forget
the key features of The Plan
that compel us to ponder and pray,
and to take advantage of the revelation
that our Father in Heaven is so anxious to
give us, which things lead us to appreciate
the Atonement, and to speedily repent of
our sins. Only then, will we discover
the happiness that has been
prepared for us.

We are
fortified by
the revelatory
reassurance that
we are the nobility
of heaven. We are as
Bagheera, the powerfully
built black panther in "The
Jungle Book," who confided to
Mowgli the man-cub: "I had never
seen the jungle. They fed me behind
bars from an iron pan till one night I
felt that I was Bagheera the Panther, and
no man's plaything, and I broke the lock
with one blow of my paw and came
away." (Rudyard Kipling).

Those who
are zipping right
along in the fast lane
of life can far too easily
blow right past celestial sign
posts that might have alerted
them, with revelatory thunder,
to move over into the exit lane
that leads to heaven's gate. For
those who do, there will come a
day when the sun shall not go
down, "neither shall the moon
withdraw itself. For the Lord
shall be their everlasting
light." (Isaiah 60:20).

Revelation
blesses us with
the knowledge that
mortality is only a tiny
fraction of a much larger
reality. It is only when we
believe it to be the sum and the
substance of our existence is our
perspective faulty. When we cannot
acknowledge the stability of the divine
center of faith, and we fail to make the
revelatory expenditure of energy to
cultivate its sense of permanency,
everything tends to collapse
into disarray.

The Spirit throws open the windows of our souls to let in more light, so that we might better understand the principles that drive God's kingdom forward. These are mysteries to those who have not prepared themselves for the streams of revelation that come from Him. The Lord has assured us, however, that we "shall know of a surety that these things are true, for from heaven will (He) declare it" unto us. (D&C 5:12).

When we prostrate
ourselves upon the altar of
faith at the feet of the Savior
with sincere questions that have
been on our minds, we will find
ourselves hovering at the edge of
forever. We will leap into a stream
of revelation, to be carried along
in a quickening current that is
nothing less than our personal
experience with God. It is by
the Spirit that we discover
the stars in heaven to
take our bearings
on eternity.

Brigham Young taught that we will have revelation from the heavens to know our forefathers "clear back to Father Adam and Mother Eve, and we will enter into the temples of God and officiate for them." Then, we will be sealed to each other until the chain is made perfect all the way from the beginning of time until its end, and we will be one happy family again.

If we
try to define
heaven and earth by
subtraction, rather than by
addition, we are destined to
fail. God's reality is infinitely
richer and more satisfying than any
poor substitute a rational approach
might grudgingly concede could
exist. The revelation we receive
from our Father is a numerical
sum that is far more than we
could ever hope to know by
relying upon nothing more
than the corruptible
lenses of our
bodies.

It is simply our honesty with ourselves as well as with God's holy Spirit that will test the mettle of our convictions. Through our acceptance of the revelation that proceeds from the mouth of God, we cast our lot with the righteous. But we have no proof until we act on the basis of trust. Then, comes the confirmation of the reality as feelings of self-confidence grow and purposeful actions replace tentative overtures. In effect, we let go and let God. We are as clay in the hands of the Master Potter.

If we
want to open
our hearts to the
spirit of revelation, we
will maintain an unbridled
optimism, and will be consumed,
as it were, by a divine fire. We will
be faithful, or full of faith. When the
Pharisees gathered together, Jesus asked
them to put revelation to its ultimate test.
He simply inquired of them, "What think
ye of Christ?" and "Whose son is he?"
(Matthew 22:41). Those questions
are ever before us, as well.

It
may be
revelation
from God that
causes our blood to
run hot, reminiscent of
the microwave background
radiation from the creation
of our universe that occurred
billions of years ago, as well
as of the creation within the
Garden of Eden, that was
not so very long ago.

The more we
think about Christ,
the easier it is to craft
with words the sensations
that naturally flow to each
of us as a result of the stirrings
of personal revelation. It becomes
that much easier to generate, and
sustain, the faith to believe in
the Father, the Son, and
the Holy Ghost.

If we want
to develop the
faith to open our
hearts to revelation, we
must expend soul-sweat. As
Robert Frost wrote: "I shall be
telling this with a sigh somewhere
ages and ages hence: Two roads
diverged in a wood, and I took
the one less traveled by, and
that has made all the
difference."

The
kingdom of God
is growing rapidly in
the Last Days. As it does
so, the Lord wants each of us
to serve in individual capacities.
Even as we recognize and appreciate
our unique qualities, experiences, and
talents, there is a revelatory bond that
brings us all together in ways that bridge
the cultural chasms that might otherwise
separate us into competing factions. We
are mystically united, and the bonds
of family makes us one.

The holy
priesthood of
God energizes His
grace as the Sacrament
is administered, allowing us
to receive blessings by binding
us to Him thru revelation by the
means of a covenant of action.
Because Heavenly Father honors
the principle of free will, our
progression patiently waits
upon our initiative. The
promise of the Spirit
of faith is ever
before us.

When we
isolate ourselves
from sensitivity to our
surroundings, we become
numb to our circumstances,
in the sense that we may very
well be past feeling. On the other
hand, as our sense of wonder in the
revelatory capacity of God is nurtured,
we realize how heavily we have borrowed
from the examples of those who have been
our sensible chaperones, our compassionate
critics, our mystical mentors, our spiritual
guides, and our surrogate saviors. These
help our heartstrings to be caressed
by the spirit of revelation with
an other-worldly vibrancy.

The level
of our faith
must be elevated
to something more
dynamic than a simple
mechanical observance of
a multiplicity of ceremonial
rules. Revelation introduces a
new element into the equations
that define the religions of our
day. For the stability of revelation
to prevail, opposition must exist as
the basis of a matrix of mayhem,
within which the fiery darts
of the adversary trace an
incendiary trail of
disorder.

Revelation is a conduit of heavenly energy that streams forth from the doorstep of the Gods. It provides stability in a world that has become befuddled by weights and measures that have been contaminated by the evidence tampering of the adversary. It not only liberates us from sin, but it also frees us from incarceration to confusion, hesitation, skepticism, ignorance, mistrust, uncertainty, suspicion, doubt, and worry.

Among
the terrible
consequences of the
world's fascination with
Babylon, and of its adoption
of the lifestyle of Beelzebub, is
spiritual insensitivity that is born
of competition between individuals.
Win or lose is the prevailing standard.
Zero sum game is the rule of play. While
business teaches that we don't get what we
deserve; instead we get what we negotiate,
in revelation, we realize that appeasement,
mediation, concession, compromise, and
arbitration are conspicuously absent.
We only see the work and glory
of God quietly in action.

The
revelations
of God carry
us in positive and
meaningful ways to
green pastures where we
enjoy the warm embrace of
the Good Shepherd, and where
we are permitted to experience
the intimacy of the touch of His
garment, even if we sometimes
feel that we have been lost
in the press of the crowd
within the sheepfold.

After
we pass
thru the portal
of baptism, our lives
open up in an expansion
of eternal opportunities as
we obtain a remission of sins,
gain membership in the Church,
and are personally sanctified by
the revelatory experiences that we
discover are embedded within our
relationship with the Holy Ghost.
In a very real sense, the Spirit
of God is with us.

We are
steadfast in our
worship of God. We
begin to comprehend
eternity, and we are of
a sound understanding. We
diligently search the scriptures,
that we might recognize the words
of truth. Thru fasting and prayer, we
have the spirit of prophecy, and we
receive revelation; and when we
teach, we do so by virtue of
the power and authority
of God.

At the Bar of Justice, the evidence will be presented, and our previous acceptance of the principles of The Plan of Salvation will determine our reward. Our innate capacity to generate faith, with the thrust being provided by the Holy Ghost in a stream of revelation, transforms the commandments into blessings. And so, once again, Heavenly Father stacks the deck in our favor.

As imperfect mortals who are struggling to believe what we do not see, the reward of our maturing faith is to see what we believe. Some things need to be witnessed in a revelatory firestorm of the Spirit, when our eyes are opened to understand the things of God, and our faith is perfected.

"We speak, not in the words which man's wisdom teacheth, but which the Holy Ghost teacheth." (1 Corinthians 2:13). These are the powerful revelations of God that permit us to brush up against the face of God to "gentle our condition," as King Henry V would say. (Shakespeare).

We
are given
the gift of the
Holy Ghost after
our baptisms, but often
we leave it unopened in its
original packaging. We forget
just how revelation will always be
there to help us make our important
choices as we engage the principles of
God's Plan. The defining characteristics
of those who embrace His revelations are the
result of their spiritual transformation when
they live, to the best of their ability, the
celestial law of the Lord, our Savior,
Jesus Christ, Who is the way, the
truth, and the life.

It is for our benefit that we become acquainted with evil as well as with good, with pain as well as with pleasure, with darkness as well as with light, with error as well as with truth, and with punishment for the infraction of God's eternal laws, as well as with the blessings that follow our obedience. Revelation is always there for us when things get rough during these character-building experiences.

Revelation
frees us from
the mire of our
unbelief, to stand
on the firm footing
that is Gospel sod. It
separates us from those
who precariously hop about
on the flotsam and jetsam
that tosses to and fro, and
bobs up and down, on the
unpredictable sea
of life.

Revelation
promises us not
just nurturing rain,
but also the mud that
must inevitably follow. It
is our lot in life to dutifully
trudge along past potholes and
other obstacles on rocky roads
that are uphill most of the way
and that face into a steady
and unrelenting headwind.
God's counsel can help
us to endure these
trials.

Revelation
from our Father
helps us to have backs
that have become sturdy
enough to brace us against
the fierce winds of adversity
and the wiles of the adversary,
and hearts that are receptacles
of pure and virtuous principles
upon which we may draw
in every time of need.

God
provides us
with an intuitive
comprehension of
where we came from,
a tangible awareness of
why we are here, and the
revelatory reassurance of
where we are going. The Plan
of God, His great and eternal
purposes, have been dramatically
communicated in revelation that
was formulated from before
the foundation of the
world.

Revelation
envelops us in
a shower of divinely
directed diamond dust
that glitters with thousands
of points of light, perceived
on earth as reflections from
above. The Spirit teaches us
that we are God's chosen
people, living within His
embrace, and enjoying
a security that others
cannot know.

The world
is at a loss for
diagnosis, even as we
are sustained by our faith
that the heavens are open, and
that our Heavenly Father, His Son
Jesus Christ, and the Holy Ghost will
provide a virtual war chest of therapies
for our cold, stony, and hard hearts. The
providential guidance that we receive
from above is the remedy of choice
for our reconciliation with
revealed religion.

In our
day, there are so
many competing voices
that can get in the way of
the revelation that we receive
thru the power of the Holy Ghost.
Insight, intuition, and inspiration are
fundamental to the implementation of
the principles, doctrines, ordinances, and
covenants of The Plan of Salvation. These
stand out in sharp contrast to the gross
darkness that so frequently shrouds
the minds of the people.
(See D&C 112:23).

Of the principles of the Gospel, Joseph Smith wrote: "This is good doctrine. It tastes good. I can taste the principles of eternal life, and so can you. They are given to me by the revelations of Jesus Christ; and I know that ... you believe them. I can taste the spirit of eternal life. I know it is good, and when I tell you of these things which were given me by inspiration of the Holy Spirit, you are bound to receive them as sweet."

In a
vain attempt
to avoid societal
implosion, and for
the sake of cultural
expediency, the target has
been moved so many times
to score repetitive bulls-eyes,
that no-one will concede that
what is really happening is that
it is actually the arrow of faith
that has strayed far from the
mark that is the revelation
of our Heavenly Father.

When we
are steadfast
in our worship, we
enjoy a knowledge of
the truth, and we are of
a sound understanding; we
search the scriptures diligently,
that we might recognize the word
of the Lord. Because we fast and we
pray, we have the spirit of prophecy,
and of revelation, and when we
teach, we do so with the power
and authority of God.
(Sew Alma 17:2-3).

As we
ascend
the ladder
of faith, rung
by rung, we will
see lightnings and
mountains smoking,
and hear loud thunder,
experiencing revelation in
its elemental forms. We will
hear the voice of trumpets
that speak in a language
that is inarticulate and
yet irrefutable.

Revelation
provides a shield
of protection against
the corrosive spatter of
perspiration cast off by the
destroyer, who pervasively and
persistently is working overtime to
damage our doctrinal defenses, dull
our spiritual sensitivities, diminish
our charitable capacity, deplete
our bountiful reservoirs of
sympathy, and destroy
our devotions.

If
we ignore
the celestial
phenomenon of
revelation from God
that is the only homing
beacon bright enough to
penetrate the swirling mists
of darkness in our telestial
world, we have tacitly chosen
an alternative course leading
to our destruction, as we run
aground on the rocky coasts
of faithlessness.

Ever since the Fall, Satan has enjoyed a free pass to mingle among the children of men. This flushes him with excitement, because he knows how difficult it is for us to resist a natural tendency toward volatility that neutralizes the spirit of revelation. Those who love Satan more than they love God, unavoidably exhibit the behavioral manifestations of that misplaced adoration, as they walk in the dark, the blind leading the blind.

Revelation
is the great equalizer,
and it treats all of us as one, no
matter in what privileged ecclesiastical
country club we may be members, or upon
what narrow theological terrace we may have
paused to catch our breath. All we really need
to do is to apply the gifts of insight, intuition,
inspiration, discernment, and revelation. All of
these are the spiritual equivalent of dusting for
the dirty fingerprints of the Devil on the idols
with which he teases, taunts, tempts, troubles,
torments, and tortures us. If we disregard
the invitation from the Spirit to heed the
counsel of God, it will be much easier
for the Devil to twist the focus of
our attention from the truth,
to his persuasive lies.

Revelation asks us to examine what it means to be anxiously engaged, inspires us to plumb the depths of our commitment to Christ, and sensitizes us to the nobility of His work. It expands upon His visions of immortality, personalizes the Atonement, and helps us to remain aware of our close proximity to eternal life. Our best intentions may be noble, but vision without work is dreamery, and even if we work hard, without vision, it is drudgery. If we focus our faith and we work with vision, however, and if we are open and receptive to communication from the heavens, it will be our destiny to soar with eagles, rather than walk with turkeys.

To
those who are
unfamiliar with
journeys thru harsh
environments, palms
often seem to grow in
desert wastes. It is only
upon closer inspection that
oases of underlying currents
of life-sustaining water may be
noticed, that bring nourishment to
the roots of the thirsty trees. So, too,
the Gospel is a storehouse of bread,
and a reservoir of living water. Its
flowing fountains of revelation
provide sustenance to all who
hunger and thirst after
righteousness.

We take
it for granted
that our prophets, our
seers, and our revelators
receive the counsel of God.
But isn't it wonderful when the
sound of the voice of the Lord
that is so familiar to them is
for us a continuous melody
and a thunderous appeal
as we faithfully serve in
lesser capacities, in
the Church and
Kingdom?

No wonder that
it is the priest's duty
to preach, teach, expound,
exhort, and to baptize, as well
as to administer the sacrament.
(See D&C 20:46). Their awesome
responsibility is to speak with faith
by the spirit of revelation as if their
voices were the Lord's own voice,
and then to follow up their
words with actions.

Revelation puts the day to day elements of The Plan in perspective, that we might more clearly be able to distinguish the grey toned obstacles that obstruct our path. These barriers to our progression will then stand out in sharp contrast against the polychromatic backdrop of the design that God has created for each one of us.

When instinct,
insight, impulse, intuition,
inspiration, and in particular,
the powerful impressions that we
receive as revelation, streak across
the heavens to find their way into
our hearts, we lift up our eyes to
follow their flaming trajectory.
Across a cosmic ocean, these
influences trace a path that
pulses with luminosity
and leads to the
doorway of the
Gods.

The temple is consecrated to be a revelatory observatory. When we look up at the stars, we are able to see things as they really are, through the clarifying lens of eternity. The aura within the Lord's holy house is crystal clear, and its uncontaminated atmosphere blesses us to be able to discern between right and wrong, and between good and evil; in short, to make choices that are based on celestial certainties, without the distortion of worldly pollution.

John F. Kennedy famously declared: "We choose to do things, not because they are easy, but because they are hard. Our goals will serve to organize and measure the best of our energies and skills. Our challenges are those that we are willing to accept, that we are unwilling to postpone, but that we intend to win." That is well put, but we must never forget that one plus God equals a majority. We need to keep the focus of our faith on His revelations, so that when we are figuratively tapped on the shoulder to do a very special thing, we will be both prepared and qualified for our finest hour.

As we
profess our
faith, the Lord
encourages us to
move forward in the
spirit of revelation, but
not in the press of a crowd
that jostles for position in the
three-ring circus of telestial trivia
that is nothing but a doctrinal dead
end, a conceptual cul-de-sac, and
and a temporal tempest. We can
not allow ourselves to become
distracted as we negotiate
the minefields of
mortality.

We must
watch ourselves
judiciously, and be
the meticulous guardians
of our thoughts, the scrupulous
custodians of our words, and the
prudent caretakers of our actions.
We fastidiously observe the laws of
God, that we might benefit from the
stability of a pathway that basks in
the steady illumination that has
been generously provided by
the spirit of revelation.

When we hunger
and thirst after a
comprehension of true
principles, and come to
the Savior anticipating a
spiritual feast, the doctrine
of the priesthood will distill
upon our souls as dews from
heaven, the Holy Ghost will be
our constant companion, and
by the power of revelation we
may discern the truth
of all things.

Revelation
has the capacity to
become the fundamental
element of a tapestry whose
intricate design will reveal itself,
in all its glory, as an expression of
God's will. "And whatsoever (we) shall
speak when moved upon by the Holy Ghost
shall be ... the will of the Lord, shall be the
mind of the Lord, shall be the word of the
Lord, shall be the voice of the Lord, and
the power of God unto salvation."
(D&C 68:4).

Since there
is opposition in
all things, even as there
is revelation, so must there
be its worldly counterpart. In
our day, the grip of fear paralyzes
many of God's children. Today, more
than ever, we need to know His mind and
will concerning our future and our fortunes.
We need His assurance of peace, that our lives
are moving forward in the direction of our
dreams, and that with His guidance, we
can reach for the stars. We need to
know that His is here, and that
we are not alone.

If we wish to
know the mind and
will of God, we must reach
out and grasp the golden rings
of insight, intuition, inspiration, and
revelation that are prominent features
as we ride along on the carousel of life.
When we exercise faith to experience for
ourselves the two way communication that
can exist between ourselves and heaven, we
move from dependence and independence,
to a stimulating interconnected revelatory
relationship with our Heavenly Father, His
Son Jesus Christ, and the Holy Ghost.
Our thoughts and feelings relating
to how we receive revelation will
stand revealed as our innocent
attempts to yoke emotions
and spiritual intuitions
to language.

The
coat of
many colors
that was worn by
Joseph is a metaphor
for the fabric of faith,
that has been sewn by our
Heavenly Father and enriched,
not by pigment and dye, but by
the revelation of His word and of
His Son. We visualize how each of its
threads has been individually tailored
to suit our circumstances; to represent,
not the drab monotone of the world,
but a veritable Technicolor Dream
Coat; one that signifies the glories
and the riches of dazzling
eternal worlds.

A
pure form of
focus transforms
our five natural senses
into something wonderful by a
heaven-sent and revelatory sixth
sense that defies description. Physical
and spiritual resources work in tandem
to compound each other, and to condition
us through the patience of faith, the miracle
of repentance, the diligence of baptism, and
the sweet sustaining spirit of the Holy Ghost,
to create an amalgamation known as the
whole armor of God.

Revelation
charges the air
in the theater of life
as fire in the sky, with an
electricity that represents an
inevitable merger between the
universal encouragement of the
Light of Christ and the pointed
and providential guidance of
the Holy Ghost. Those who
are firm in their faith in
the script of The Plan
will find heaven, as
it knocks at their
door asking for
a curtain
call.

As would be
expected, revelation,
nurtures our relationship
with God and the Holy Ghost.
We become the fashioners of our
fortunes as we learn to rely upon
reserves that are only found in
our Savior, Jesus Christ. We
realize that His wisdom is
infinitely greater than
our understanding
of everything.

As we listen
to the Holy Ghost,
all that we must do will
be revealed in spectacular
simplicity and plainness. The
Spirit will comfort and succor
us with the bread of life. As we
journey through the harsh and
unforgiving environment of
Idumea, seeking the Lord
while He may be found,
oases will spring up
in the desert and
living water will
slake our
thirst.

It is only through the
uninterrupted intervention
and attention by our Father
in Heaven, His Son Jesus Christ,
and the Holy Ghost, that mortality
can become the wonderful revelatory
learning center for the talented and
gifted that it was envisioned to be
even before the world was made.
Surely the Lord God will do
nothing, without revealing
His secret to those whom
we esteem as His
prophets and
seers.

Revelation
forges a spiritual
bond between ourselves
and our fellow travelers,
and our Father in Heaven,
by obedience that is more
expansive than a law of
carnal commandments.
It requires the inter-
dependency of
the greater
law.

When we have been touched by the spirit of revelation, and we begin to grasp the nature of The Plan of Salvation and how it was conceived, we learn more about how we fit in to God's divine design. We learn how faith can drive the law into our inward parts. When it does so, the articles of our faith become the particles of our faith.

Knowing
that we can be
guided by revelation
influences us to be more
trusting and to speak without
guile. We are more transparent
and are less prejudicial. We have
fewer pretensions and are more
genuine. We are less prone to
rationalization and quicker
to forgive. We are more
likely to greet others
with a warm "Hello
Neighbor!" as did
Mr. Rogers.

Guidance that we
receive from our Father
in Heaven helps us to clearly
identify the fingerprints of the
adversary when they have been
smeared all over a plethora of
penurious programs, policies,
politics, and parties that do
little more than to promote
personal, and provincial
proclamations relating
to plans that are, at
best, petty.

Revelation helps us
to focus on what God wants
to happen, instead of allowing
ourselves to be distracted by what
we don't want to happen. Revelation
helps us to envision success so that
the conclusion will be foregone. It
sends a reassuring message to all
of God's children that it is their
destiny to enjoy dancing with
the stars of heaven, and it
outlines the ways for
them to do so.

The compromise of
our trust that our Father
in Heaven speaks to us in a
revelatory thunder, if and when
He wishes to do so, can be traced
to the lack of a faithful focus that
initiated the flat spin from which we
couldn't recover. We may be tempted
to assign the blame for the demolition
of our discipleship and the cascade of
negative consequences that follows at
the doorstep of others, but sooner or
later, it will come home to roost
at our own threshold.

Those who
are bound by revelation
take commitment to a new
level. They redefine dedication.
They exercise their duties in ways
that are truly selfless. The Gospel has
transformed their lives. They are as the
people of Zarahemla, who declared to
King Benjamin: "The Spirit of the Lord
Omnipotent ... has wrought a mighty
change in us, or in our hearts, that
we have no more disposition to
do evil, but (instead, it is
our heartfelt desire) to
do good continually."
(Mosiah 5:2).

In our obedience,
we try to be perfect in
our repentance, that God
might give unto us the spirit
of wisdom and of revelation,
to enlighten our understanding,
that we might embrace the hope of
the high calling of our Savior Jesus
Christ, and that the riches of glory
might abide, through the grace of
God, as our unmerited
inheritance.

When we
have revelation
to guide us, we know
how to worship and we
know what to worship, for
truth may be recognized by
its effects. We test the claims
of the Gospel by rendering
unswerving obedience to
its principles of
action.

A society
that denies God
the power to speak,
deals with its spiritual
myopia with a knee-jerk
reaction that simply ratchets
down its expectations. In the
end, if a culture lacks the fire
of faith, it will ask pitifully
little of heaven, and will
necessarily receive
in kind.

It is our faith that
teaches us to face the sun,
that we may feel the warmth
of its rays upon our cheeks, listen
with greater sensitivity, hear the word
of the Lord without ambiguity, and see
with a lucidity that encourages us to
drop to our knees in thanksgiving to
God for His benevolence, and for
opening up the heavens in a
revelatory rapture of
divine direction.

It is our faith in the revealed word of our Heavenly Father that commits us to the arduous process of the spiritual rebirth that accompanies our choice of life and light. To neglect to do so would be a capitulation to the miscarriage that is death and darkness. Fear is character crippling. It can be devastating to the capacity of our listening ears to be able to recognize truth when the Holy Ghost speaks to us by the power of faith.

Revelation
from our Father,
Who dwells within the
fire of eternal glory and in
everlasting burnings, explains
how to have lips that articulate
uplifting expressions that would
never speak guile, and shoulders
that have developed the strength
to bear the burdens of those who
have been battered and bruised
by the vicissitudes of life and
who may be faltering under
the heavy weight of sorrow
or unresolved sin.

Those with faith
will hunger and thirst
after righteousness. They
are filled with the spirit of
revelation that comes from the
Holy Ghost. They press forward
with dedication, feasting on the
scriptures. They receive physical
and spiritual nourishment, and
they endure to the end with
continuing responsibility
and accountability.

How many times have we read about, or even witnessed, cultural collapse because a faithless society has decayed from within? In every case, iniquity follows those who yield themselves "unto the power of Satan." (3 Nephi 7:5). Some people do not seem to be able to understand that Lucifer was a first-grade dropout whose influence was the companion of anarchy because it not only denied revelation, but also because it demeaned even the intelligent application of knowledge.

It is nothing less than our faith that binds together the building blocks of eternal principles. Without faith, the fabric of our lives unravels in a process leading to disintegration. If the anchor of revelation from heaven is absent, our experiences can be like a train wreck in slow motion that will be frustratingly repeated, over and over, in a monotonous repetition.

As we fine-tune
our revelatory capabilities,
we can build upon experiences
with the Holy Ghost that we have
already had, that come to us as
we patiently wait upon The Plan.
These include our testimonies of
Jesus Christ and of His Gospel,
of the divine authenticity of
The Book of Mormon, and
of the mission of
Joseph Smith.

If we
will not listen
to the promptings of
the Holy Ghost, we cannot
reasonably expect to inherit
the glory of celestial realms;
especially if we have aforetime
been agreeable to only abide by
telestial or terrestrial principles
that put fewer demands upon
our discipleship, or upon
our capacity to receive
revelation from
God.

Neglect of
our spiritual health
in any degree whatsoever
requires the implementation
of sweeping counter-measures.
The plastic surgery of repentance
is prompted by the Holy Ghost, and is
indicated if we want to experience the
reversal of our fortunes; if we would
like to be on the receiving end of a
revelatory exchange with God, to
exhibit, in a coming day, both
His likeness and image in
our countenances.

Faith in our Father in
Heaven, light from above, and
eternal truth are the trifecta of
revelation, and are recognized as
irreducible common denominators.
They are the essential elements of an
equation that describes the foundation
upon which knowledge is received. "One
for all and all for one!" was the motto
of the Three Musketeers. Without faith,
light, and truth, said Joseph Smith,
we would retrogress, "degenerate
from God, descend to the devil,
and lose knowledge," and
without it we cannot
be saved.

Our faith
pushes us onward
and upward, which often
means that we persevere to
the point that we feel that we
have no more to give. It is at the
point of utter exhaustion that we
must turn to powers that are
greater than ourselves, to
the revelation of God,
if we hope to survive
the fall.

Innumerable
gurus have guided
our lives with a profound
influence that has helped us
to nurture the tender feelings
that have helped us to shape
our capacity to receive the
revelations of God, and
then to act upon our
inspiration from
above.

Our redemption
requires that we establish a
familiarity with revelation from
Him Who is the Way, the Truth, and
the Life. We must find ways to have
direct experience with God, with Jesus
Christ and with the Holy Ghost. We are
charged with an infinite perspective, to
experience a pulsing stream of insight,
intuition, inspiration, and revelation
whose mighty flow has no spatial
and no temporal boundary.

Whenever we
have unknowingly
taken poetic license with
the foundation principles of
The Plan, or if we have added
needless ecclesiastical embroidery
to the truth we receive by the spirit
of revelation, we diminish our faith
to believe. The only remedy that
is available to us is to speedily
repent and wrap ourselves in
the simple cross-stitch of
Gospel principles.

Revelation reacquaints us with the divine design of God that puts the finishing touches on our dissertation on life. As we are perfected, our composition will be recognized for what it has become: God's magnum opus, even His work and glory.

Because it is easy to talk about revelation in timid or shallow ways, by retreating into insipid and colorless verbiage as an easy way out, we take care that we have not steered a course that might take us away from the Savior with inconsiderate, dismissive, or offhand expressions.

Jesus
encouraged
us to give ourselves
completely and without
reservation, that we might
enjoy a state of harmony with
Him and synchronization with the
eternities. He asked us to search
without ceasing, that we might
discover within revelation
the divine center of
our faith.

Those of us
who have the faith to
become the beneficiaries
of God's divine revelation,
have been touched by angels
to walk along pathways that
have been illuminated by
by the stunning light
of the Lord.

Today, our society which is arguably good, has utterly failed to instill within the rising generation any appreciation of God's revelatory capacity. When a culture believes that truth is relative and that the merits of faith are arbitrarily determined without the need for heavenly intervention, the stage has been set for a disaster of biblical proportion.

As the seasons
of our lives unfold
before us, we realize how
much we need the influence of
the Holy Ghost and to engage in the
revelatory process. "For life is a sheet
of paper white, where each of us may
write a line or two, and then comes
night. Greatly begin! If thou hast
time for but a line, make that
sublime. Not failure, but
low aim, is crime."
(James Lowell).

Our Father in Heaven is bursting with excitement to reveal many important things that pertain to His Kingdom. He sends us tenderly composed 'letters' of encouragement, hoping that we will receive and read them with enthusiasm. Faint lines of communication from the Spirit are nurtured to become avenues of correspondence that freely flow between heaven and earth.

Those of weak will, who turn away from the promptings of the Holy Ghost that come to us as revelations from God, lose their focus, just as eyesight may be lost over time. First they squint, and then they hold the page a little closer or a little further away, compensating for the inability to see clearly. Whether it is the printed page or their integrity that they cannot read, if they lose the Spirit, there will be a demoralizing crash of conscience and a character crippling compromise, in a free-fall from faith.

When cultural
collapse is imminent,
external controls are often
imposed to manipulate behavior,
to maintain at least a semblance
of societal steadiness. Our escalating
dependence on laws to regulate moral
discipline says something about us, and
about our critical need for faith that
God speaks to us, at His pleasure,
about matters that are of great
importance to both of us.

The
world seeks to
change us by exerting
external controls, but it
fails miserably. The Savior
makes change by transforming
the inner vessels, and succeeds
brilliantly. He goes about doing
this by calibrating our internal
sextants, so that we may take
our bearings on the guiding
stars of revelation from
the heavens.

It is heartbreaking when
those who have matriculated
in the curriculum of the Gospel,
but cannot sustain saving faith in
revelatory instruction from God, set
their sights too low, too easily reaching
watered-down objectives. They no longer
stretch themselves, and rarely venture out
of the comfort zones to which they have
retreated. They have little to show for
their consistently timid efforts that
deny the faith but that have, by
their actions, become habitual
in their expression.

All of us
are repeatedly
faced with occasions
when withdrawals must be
made from our spiritual bank
accounts. When we respond to the
Spirit, Who drives us to our knees to
seek the revelatory word of the Lord,
we appreciate the regular deposits that
have already been made for us. We then
are able to rely upon the cornucopia of
comfort created by the cushion of
confidence that is a currency
flowing from conduct that
is consistent with the
core curriculum of
contrition.

Every time we think in
rational terms, we seem to be
hedged in by the very things from
which we yearn to be free: our mortal
perspective and perceptions, that are, sad
'tho it seems, the sum and substance of our
temporal experiences. Because of the Light of
Christ, we are all intuitively drawn to seek the
right answers, but if we do not also receive
revelation, which is the further light and
knowledge that the Lord has promised
to give to us, we will be condemned
to ask the wrong questions, and
to do so habitually.

Those who undertake to grapple with the permutations and combinations of revelation realize that the key of knowledge may be employed by both those who are in poverty and those who abound in wealth. It is engaged by both fame and obscurity, exercised in sickness and in health, put to good use by those with influence as well as by those who are living in anonymity, and it may be successfully retained by both beauty and the beast.

Through
the workings of the
spirit of revelation, and by
the power of our faith, we see all
the way to heaven, with the capacity
to be carried beyond the perceptible
and palpable confines of this world
to a place where boundaries are
blurred, and the barricade of
borders evaporates in a
flood of light.

In a sharp contrast to the hectic demands that are put upon us by the world, revelation quietly generates repetitive opportunities for us to stop and smell the roses along the way, during our journey Home. In fact, our Heavenly Father created the roses in the first place, as 'love letters' to His children. Of these subtle reinforcements, Elizabeth Barrett Browning wrote: "Earth is crammed with heaven, and every bush with fire of God. But only those who see, take off their shoes. The rest stand around picking blackberries."

It is never enough merely to have been given the gift of the Holy Ghost and to have the spirit of revelation. If we do nothing with them, and coast to a standstill before we have made our way to the feet of the Savior, we are at risk of toppling over. Our forward momentum needs to be maintained if we are to keep our balance as we follow His footsteps.

The revelation
that is so freely given
by our Heavenly Father is
everywhere. It is an engine that
runs best when it operates between
the hot reservoir of the Son and the
cold reaches of outer space. With its
equilibrium, we may recognize, address,
reverse, and erase for once and for
all, the imbalance that so easily
can creep into our lives.

Perhaps
we embrace revelation
because we have discovered
that it is only by establishing
communication with God that we
receive transfusions of the spiritual
element. It is as a heavenly dialysis
machine, where worldly contaminants
are removed from our systems because
we are incapable of accomplishing the
task on our own. The resources we
need may only be found in the
correspondence that exists
between ourselves and
the heavens.

An uninterrupted
flow of revelation liberates us
to enjoy God's peace, to receive
the blessings of the priesthood, to
serve others in more powerful and
significant ways, to resolutely work
toward our potential, to commune
with the Infinite, and to benefit
from all of the other blessings
of The Plan of Salvation, as
we move forward into
eternity.

Faith invites us to enjoy the sweet influence of the Holy Ghost, Who, as a revelatory creative consultant, is always ready to volunteer His constructive comments that relate to our developing story board. We realize that it is with the testimony of Jesus, or the spirit of prophecy, that personal revelation can bring all of Heavenly Father's children to the knowledge of His Plan; to their own independent testimony of the Savior, and to faith in His Atonement.

Revelation
draws upon the
magnificent power
of all three members
of the Godhead, so that
we may become increasingly
receptive to flashes of insight.
We are cast off into streams of
inspiration that carry us along
in the quickening currents of
direct experience with our
Heavenly Father, with
Jesus Christ and
with the Holy
Ghost.

When, as we
receive revelation,
our passions cloud our
vision and overpower our
zealous intentions, or if we
appear to drift over the line
separating true doctrine from
baseless speculation, we ask
the forgiving indulgence of
our Father in Heaven, the
sustaining influence of
the Spirit, and our
own patience
of faith.

When we
overlook the
revelatory influence
of the Holy Ghost that
nurtures our innate urge to
abhor mischief, but instead allow
ourselves to be habitually distracted
by trifling concerns until they become
the center of our attention and even our
obsession, we ignore our innate yearning
to exercise saving faith in our Heavenly Father,
and risk settling for life in a marshland
of mediocrity that quickly degenerates
into the quicksand of sin, from
which, quite simply, there is
no easy escape.

It makes no
difference if we
look to the right or
to the left, because the
Savior is always there. When
we lift our eyes to the heavens,
He is watching us from above. No
matter that we bear the weight of
sin or sorrow with downcast eyes;
He is always beneath us, to lift
us up and carry our burdens.
The universe is pulsing with
inspiration and is alive
with the revelations
of God.

We have
faith that Jesus
is the Father of our
spiritual regeneration,
and like the parent we all
aspire to be, He will be there
to bind our wounds and heal
our infirmities every time we
stumble and whenever we fall
because of the weight we have
been trying to carry all by
ourselves. Though we may
disregard the Revelation
of God, He will never
ignore us.

"Read yourselves full, think yourselves straight, pray yourselves hot, and let yourselves go!" (Douglas Gibb). The first three admonitions involve faithful preparation. They set the stage for purposeful action, to 'let ourselves go' as we listen for the peaceful revelatory counsel of the Spirit of the Lord.

Each of us can be
blessed with a witness
that we receive through
personal revelation, to be
sanctified in Christ by the
grace of God, and through
the shedding of His blood,
which is in the covenant
of the Father unto the
remission of our sins.
We are consecrated
to become holy
and without
spot.

One of the
terrible consequences
of the fascination of Babylon
with telestial titillation, and with
its fixation on the vain images of
the world, is spiritual insensitivity
to the revelation it might have
received, if it had expressed
even a remote interested
in learning about The
Plan of God.

The Lord selects those
who are humble and worthy,
and then He tutors them through
the power of the Holy Ghost and the
influence of The Plan of God, revealing
His will unto them. Those whom He selects
are "the weak things of the world." (D&C 1:19).
As President Kimball once stated: "Christianity
did not go from Rome to Galilee. It was
the other way around. In our day, the
routing is from Palmyra to Paris,
and not the reverse."

When
we enjoy
an unrestrained
rapport with God,
our faith to act will
generate the power to
'get things done' in an
expansive and interactive
way, in all holiness. We will
recognize His revelatory voice
as the Spirit of truth, which
"abideth and hath no end.
And if it be in (us) it
shall abound."
(D&C 88:66).

The
Revelation of
God can save us
from our natural state
of carnality, sensuality, and
devilish inclinations. It can lift us
to angelic innocence, and help us to
feel comfortable as we prepare to return
to our heavenly home, to find ourselves in
in the presence of angels who are singing
celestial lullabies that tangibly express
the love of our Father in Heaven.

No
wind can
blow except
it fills our sails to
carry each of us ever
closer to our destination,
without delay or interruption,
and without unnecessary cost,
loss, or sacrifice. All that is
required is that we so live
as to be worthy of the
revelations that our
Father is anxious
to give to
us.

Revelation that
comes from our Father
in Heaven provides us with a
regularly recurring reassurance
of a religious recalibration that auto
corrects with celestial precision. It can
envelop us in an intuitive appreciation of
where we came from, why we are here, and
where we are going. It gives us the courage
to face the future with confidence and
to maintain our forward momentum
during the journey so we won't
lose our balance, topple over,
and possibly damage our
divine nature.

Our attempts
to comprehend the
universe may help us
to understand ourselves.
If we ask, what is its origin,
or what is its ultimate destiny,
we are really asking where did we
come from, and where are we going.
When we discover the answers to these
questions, we will understand why we
are here, and we will be prepared to
embark upon a journey where our
traveling companion is the Holy
Ghost, our revelatory guide,
Who will escort us into
the future.

Guidance from above that
comes to us in the form of spiritual
promptings and subtle impressions is more
common that many would suspect. There are
powerful intuitive communicators that strongly
influence nearly all of us to push forward in
the direction of our dreams, toward a faith
to believe that blesses us with a greater
appreciation of the concern of our
Creator for each of us, and with
the power to act upon our
promptings.

When we
think of the
multitude of those
angels who are thinly
disguised as our families,
friends, and peers, who have
helped us to nurture our capacity
to receive revelation, we remember
the words of Sir Isaac Newton, who,
when pressed to reveal the secret
behind his accomplishments,
simply replied: "I stood
on the shoulders of
giants."

The originality
and resourcefulness
of the mind of God are such
that His revelations are designed
with redundant mechanisms that will
provide us with repetitive opportunities to
pause for analysis, reflection, commitment,
and renewal, while miraculously minimizing
our tendency to focus inward. As our lives
conform to His guidance, we find our
greatest expression, and self-doubt
or second-guessing is virtually
eliminated.

Before
the world was,
God determined that He
would respond to our trials and
temptations as any parent anxious
about the welfare of their children who
live away from home would do. Revelation,
as it turns out, is the best way to stay in touch
with us. He views our challenges as nothing more
than pop quizzes in the learning laboratory of
life, but it is His on-going counsel and His
direction that prepares us for the final
exam that will come shortly after
the conclusion of our mortal
curriculum.

Revelation
is the torch of truth. It
is a beacon that guides those
who are having difficulty finding
their way home. The best among those
who receive revelation for the Church
wear the heavy robes of responsibility
of God's priesthood, or operate
under its influence and
at its direction.

Those who have been
blessed with the revelatory
gift have somehow been able to
break free of "the influence of that
spirit which hath so strongly riveted
the creeds of the fathers, who have
inherited lies, upon the hearts of
the children, and filled the
world with confusion.
(D&C 123:7).

Even with
revelation, we only
dimly perceive our noble
heritage, and we sometimes
find it hard to accept the fact
that we mingled among the Gods
before our mortal births. The Hubble
telescope can 'see' 13.2 billion light
years into our past, almost back to
the moment of creation itself, but
it cannot gaze into heaven for
five minutes. Only revelation
has the capacity to do so.

Revelation
is a star map that
has been created by the
hand of God to illuminate
the pathway to the promised
land. It is an endowment of
radiant light and of unearthly
power. It is nothing short of the
revelation that comes from God,
that has the power to disperse the
darkness from before us, and
cause the heavens to shake
for our good.

Even as faith
molds us in mortality,
it establishes us in eternity.
We quickly learn to respond to the
the heavenly smiles that we recognize
as revelation, so that one day, we
might be asked to become engaged
in a heavenly inner beauty
contest.

Blind opposition, enmity, hatred, hostility, inflexibility, and intolerance are the raw manifestations of pride, but these are overwhelmed by the faith, hope, and charity of those who respond to the revelatory promptings of the Holy Ghost.

When we turn our
backs on the habitation
of the Lord, we are painting
ourselves into conceptual corners,
limiting our creative expression to a
narrow and confusing rational reality
of our own construction. When we turn
our backs to the light of revelation,
we may think we have it all, when
all that is really before us is an
illusion that is a shadow and
a caricature of reality.

Faithful participants
in life's Three Act Play are
now and forever independent in
that stage of development to which
their decisions have led them. Poised
on the edge of forever, they need little
incentive other than revelations from
God to push off into the unknown
possibilities of existence.

Those who have
forsaken the world
and have embraced the
revelations of God, experience
nothing short of a spiritual heart
transplant. Therefore, anti-rejection
protocols must be followed after
we have spiritually been given
our new hearts and have
been born again.

The Apostle Paul admonished the Saints to work out their salvation with fear and trembling; to open their hearts to spiritual promptings. He knew that to do so would leave them physically and spiritually exhausted. Still, he invited them to join him as he pressed "toward the mark, for the prize of the high calling of God in Christ Jesus." (Philippians 3:14).

There will come
for each of us a great
and dreadful day when we
will be asked to stand and give
our sworn deposition before God,
angels, and witnesses. On the issue of
our acceptance of revelation, depending
upon our answer, we will be counted
among the sheep or the goats, and
we will be asked to take our
place at His right hand
or at His left hand.

In matters
of revelation, it is not the
Lord, but we, who are on trial.
At the Bar of Justice, He will simply
weigh the facts. Our previous acceptance or
rejection of the whisperings of the Spirit will
determine our reward or our punishment.
Trial proceedings have already been
docketed to immediately follow
our mortal experience, and
they will be even-handed
and eminently
fair.

Joseph Smith
understood the spirit
of revelation when he prayed:
"Help us by the power of thy Spirit,
that we may mingle our voices with
those bright, shining seraphs around
thy throne, with acclimations of
praise, singing Hosanna to
God and the Lamb!"
(D&C 109:79).

The gate may
be strait and the
way narrow, but those
who accept the guidance
of revelation will find that it
is within their capacity to travel a
path of progression by threading the
eye of the needle and walking a fine
line past the seemingly unalterable,
unavoidable, and unstoppable
demands of disproportion
that define mortality.

We are
inspired by
revelation, that
we might "try the
virtue of the word
of God." (Alma 31:5)
We do so, that we might
reap its rewards, and with
diligence, patience, and
long-suffering, harvest
the fruit of the Tree
of Life from its
low hanging
branches.

Eternal
progression
rules supreme,
but it is defined
by its opposites in
the physical universe
just as it is by the forces
of opposition in the eternal
world. The presence of God
and the influence of Satan
in the Garden of Eden
attest to the necessity
of both revelation,
or light, and
darkness,
or sin.

The Spirit
instills within us a
sound understanding as
we search the scriptures, that
we might know the word of God.
But this is not all; we give ourselves
to prayer, and fasting, that we might
enjoy the spirit of prophecy, and the
spirit of revelation, so that when
we teach, we teach with power
and the authority of God.

Joseph Smith taught: "We may profit by noticing the first intimation of the spirit of revelation; for instance, when we feel pure intelligence flowing into us, it may give us sudden strokes of ideas ... By learning the Spirit of God and understanding it, we may grow into the principle of revelation." The Holy Ghost, then, is a schoolmaster Who is commissioned to bring us, by that same spirit of revelation, thru the doctrine of Christ into the presence of our Heavenly Father.

If we really want to receive
the blessing of the ordinances of
the Gospel, to "always have His spirit to be
with us," we need to experience how the Holy
Ghost manifests personal revelation. "For God
speaketh once, yea twice, yet man perceiveth it
not. In a dream, in a vision of the night,
when deep sleep falleth upon men, in
slumberings upon the bed; then he
openeth the ears of men, and
sealeth their instruction."
(Job 33:4-16).

We lose
the focus of
our faith that the
heavens remain open,
just as we lose the acuity
of our vision, over time. Whether
it is the letter of the law or an eye
chart that is beyond our comprehension,
we become legally blind. Having eyes,
we cannot see what is clearly
before our faces.

Revelation
from our Father
in Heaven helps us to
shun telestial temptations
that are so cunningly peddled
by the snake oil salesmen who have
set up shop in the great and spacious
buildings that dot the landscapes
of our lives, and that pop up
out of nowhere and in the
most unexpected
places.

Our covenants are binding contracts between ourselves and God, and come through revelation. No person who participates in Gospel ordinances enters into such covenants except on the basis of direct revelation from Him. It follows that the only ones who can legitimately enter into covenants are those who qualify by worthiness to participate in the sacred ordinances that have been designed to bring us into the presence of Heavenly Father, Jesus Christ, and the Holy Ghost.

Revelation may be recognized only when we have allowed ourselves to fall under the influence of the Spirit. Communications from the heavens only wait upon our initiative. So it is with all of the covenants and the ordinances of the Gospel. They are not subject to private interpretation. In a perfect storm of knowledge, belief, and faith, it is the sunlight of revelation that will switch on as a bright and shining star in the heavens, whose fuel will power the chain reaction within its celestial furnace.

Our faith
is a tool that
allows us to see
beyond the limited
horizon of our sight,
to be touched by a vision
of the virtue of the word of
God. Our faith enables us to
savor revealed truth with a
discriminating taste that
discerns the distinctive
flavor of eternal
worlds.

As we
faithfully
carry out our
work, and quietly
face our obligations,
the righteousness of our
cause will be revealed in
marvelous simplicity and in
plainness. Walls of opposition
to our progression will crumble
and fall away. The Lord Jesus
Christ will comfort us and
will succor us with the
revelatory bread
of life.

Disorder
and progression
must be in balance
with each other. It was
ordained in heaven before
the world was that there must
be a healthy juxtaposition of
forces for faith to prevail
as the first principle of
revealed religion.

When the
octane rating of the
fuel that fires our faith to
receive revelation from God
is too low, we may be able to
just barely get by, but only for a
time. We will limp along with our
engines misfiring badly, until we
finally coast to a stop in the
dead of the night in the
wintery weather of
our unbelief.

Joseph's coat was a gift from his father, just as we receive the fabric of our faith as a gift, that we might enjoy revelation. We can be certain that our Father has carefully selected every bolt of cloth and has thoughtfully cut each of them to accommodate the pattern that He has planned, to light up our lives.

We live in the midst of Spiritual Babylon, and recoil as we encounter a sprawling wasteland of worldliness that reeks of the rotting stench of sin. But we must never allow the pure and unadulterated revelation that we receive from Father in Heaven to be contaminated by the raw sewage that is unleashed by Satan's servants, who often wear the thin disguise of sanitation workers.

If we wish to gain a
testimony of the principles
of the Gospel of Jesus Christ,
we need to address three essential
elements. First, we are introduced to
the eternal principle. Second, is our
correct understanding of the Lord's
counsel concerning the principle,
and finally, is our experience
with the principle, that comes
by revelation, and is the
fruits of faith.

Belief is
the mental
assent to the
truth of a precept,
principle, or doctrine,
without the moral element
of responsibility that we call
faith. Of those to whom much is
given, however, much is expected,
and so our faith demands action.
When we move upon our spiritual
promptings, the flood-gates
of heaven are opened to
release a torrent of
revelation.

It is particularly
during times of weakness
that it may seem to us that
the easier way out is to adopt
the ways of the world. It may be
harder for us to acknowledge the
revelatory autobiographical thread
that forthrightly wends its way to
heaven. Sometimes, we cannot
see the forest for the trees,
and we forget that our
universe is a machine
for the making
of gods.

Those
with faith to
pattern their lives
around the revealed
word of God will distain
Babylons' amusement parks,
while gratefully utilizing the
aid stations that have been
providentially positioned
all over Zion, and in
particular, in the
stakes of
Zion.

To preserve
the principle of free
will, a veil has been drawn
across our minds. But we have
the spirit of revelation to help
us to penetrate that curtain. Yet,
many of us are still swayed by other
voices that ring louder in our ears; by
the siren song of Satan, we are drawn
to his duplicitous shoals of spiritual
instability, thereon to founder, and
to be pulled down by the riptides
of religious relativism and the
undertow of agnosticism, or
faithless skepticism.

If we permit our fears to overcome our faith, as well as to handcuff the expression of the spirit of revelation, all that will be left in the end is a monochromatic and one-dimensional compromise that leaves us with a hollow core of emptiness in the pit of our stomachs and terror in our hearts. Faith, after all, is fear that has said its prayers.

Even with the aid of the world's most powerful telescopes, and notwithstanding the Light of Christ, we have been privileged only to take a peek at the creations Moses beheld through the mighty power of faith, while he was under the mighty revelatory influence of the Spirit.

Wo unto those
who will only casually
receive the illumination
of revelation that has been
so freely given. Because of their
misguided obsession with temporal
trivia, they carelessly fritter away
their faith, and waste the days of
their probation rooting through
telestial trash in a fruitless
effort to find meaning
in the dumpsters of
their empty lives.

They faithful
keep their faces
oriented toward the
light, so the shadows will
always be behind them. They
rely on revelation from God to
guide them, and do not allow the
encroaching darkness to distract
them from going about their
Father's business.

Society pays
a very heavy price
when it lacks a faithful
focus on the solemnities of
eternity and on the revelations
that have been so freely proffered
to us. For example, when its spiritual
equilibrium has become so disoriented
that its moral compass is spinning out of
control, its values are quickly adjusted in
a misguided, vain, and even an unconscious
attempt to regain a state of balance
between heaven and earth.

Belittling the
belief of another person
in revelation from our Father
in Heaven requires minimal effort.
It is an avoidance of the obedience of
faith. It is a flight from responsibility,
and it ignores accountability. Someone
once said that God gave us two ends:
One to think with and the other one
to sit on. Which one we use will
determine how well we do in
life. In other words: Heads
we win, and tails we
lose.

As long as we keep the focus of attention of our faith in the revelatory ability of the Spirit to guide our lives, we won't get in the thick of thin things. We focus on the cultivation of an equilibrium that is centered far from the madding crowd, at a safe distance from the ego-filled minds of mediocre men. We are insulated from the tumult, the confusion, and the cares of the world, and enjoy a firmness that is unshakable.

The open lines of communication between ourselves and God protects us from a false sense of carnal security, as well as from indifferent complacency. We view our weaknesses in positively constructive ways, and are grateful for our conscious awareness of opportunities for personal improvement, and for the tools that we have been given to accomplish every aspect of our mortal mission assignments.

Revelation is a
part of the fabric that has
been woven by God into the
tapestry of our lives. We simply
turn to the inventory of thread that
He has provided for us in a continual
stream of new colors, that enables us
to weave imaginative patterns that
celebrate our confidence in
His divine design.

Obstacles are those frightful things that we see when we take our minds off our goals. They loom large with gratuitous significance. It is revelation that endows us with the vision to see beyond these potential stumbling blocks. It empowers us to rely upon the expansive, creative engine for positive change that is the Gospel, by turning them into stepping-stones that pave the way to higher achievement.

Among the
greatest virtues
we can have are a
well-trained mind, a
body to match, a love of
achievement, and a welcoming
heart that embraces revelation.
Without these, life can be nothing
more than smoke and mirrors,
and we grow old before
our time.

It is revelation that reintroduces us to the quiet instruction from our Heavenly Father that nurtured us during our spiritual kindergarten years in the pre-earth existence. Once again, we are blessed to walk in the light of life, as we return in our hearts to that more natural state of harmony with the heavens.

The
celestial compass of
revelation is calibrated
to be oriented toward truth,
and is always available to guide
the faithful to a safe haven. It is also
there for those who have lost their way,
to bring them into the fold of the Good
Shepherd, or to show prodigal sons how
to return to the safety and security
of the community of Christ from
which they have strayed.

Those without faith lack the
spiritual horsepower of revelation.
Their dearth of traction is obvious,
their inability to generate spontaneity
is palpable, and their lack of energy
to engage enthusiasm is noticeable.
Their incapacity to spark vitality
is evident, and their failure to
candidly acknowledge the
powerful relationship that
can exist between God
and ourselves is
undisputed.

We must
venture forth
out of our shadowy
sanctuaries, and learn
to rely upon the guidance
that we receive from the Light
of Christ and the ministering of
angels, not to mention instinct,
insight, intuition, inspiration,
and revelation, if we want
to experience the special
familiarity enjoyed by
the faithful with the
Lord of all the
earth.

The
influence of
the foundation of
faith creates a bridge
of understanding between
the secular and the divine.
Life, with all its twists and
turns, and its permutations
and combinations, suddenly
makes more sense, as we
receive revelation and
begin to understand
the mind and will
of God.

Empowered by
revelation of God,
our innermost longings
to apprehend visions of the
eternal world are epitomized
by our triumphant realization of
dreams fulfilled. In the expression
of our testimonies, our emotions are
painted by words that depict our
progression toward the distant
mileposts that mark the way
we must all follow on our
journey to heaven.

Those who
were denied the
chance in this life to
embrace the Gospel will be
judged according to their more
limited understanding of the doctrines
and principles of God's Plan. Therefore,
when they approach the Bar of Justice, they
will necessarily vary in their accountability
to law. Therein lies the hidden power of the
Holy Ghost to ultimately bless their lives.
Beside the Savior, He will become their
advocate, and He will justify them
as long as their behavior had
been in harmony with the
principles of the
Plan.

As we live in
obedience to the
covenants that we
have made with God,
we prepare ourselves thru
sanctification by the Spirit to
be led unerringly by the Lord. We
take Him at His word, when He says:
"Mine angels shall go up before you,
and also my presence." (D&C 103:20).
With the guidance that is provided by
revelation from God, it is possible
to negotiate the strait and narrow
path all the way to the Tree of
Life, there to partake of its
delicious fruit, that is a
representation of life
that is sweet and
precious.

Secular humanism and other ideologies that extoll the virtues of the intellect and demand tangible proof will ever be at odds with revelation. They destroy faith, and divert us from following the Plan whose successful execution hinges upon nourishing the seeds of innocent faith in the word of God. In the thoughtful words of Sir Walter Scott: "Better had they ne'er been born, who reads to doubt, or reads to scorn." (Sir Walter Scott).

To have the
unlimited freedom
to choose for ourselves
in an atmosphere that is so
full of dangerous deceptions,
enticing entrapments, soothing
seductions, and perilous pathways,
entails risk. Revelation introduces us
to a peaceful sanctuary that remains
remarkably untainted from the blood
and sins of this generation, where we
may flee from Babylon to faithfully
exercise our agency not only to be,
but infinitely more importantly,
to become. God's work, after
all, is to bring to pass our
immortality and eternal
lives.

Who would
consciously choose to
lead a marginalized life or
to become spiritually depleted
on a personal or an institutional
level by denying the revelations of
God? We perish because our faith has
failed us. But how many of us realize
that it really the other way around,
and that it is we who have failed
our faith? Fortunately, we are
blessed with the gift of the
Atonement, and the Savior
can change all that,
beginning right
now.

Revelation
sustains us as
we receive with
equanimity whatever
comes our way during
the incubation period of
our spiritual metamorphosis
that was designed to be just
as challenging as it would
be rewarding.

The revelation
with which we have
been blessed surprises us in
myriad and delightful ways. It
cultivates a culture of reflection,
keeps the Savior in our thoughts,
nurtures an eternal perspective,
initiates positive change, and
harmonizes our behavior
with His charitable
example.

Far too many
of us, by seeking the
approbation of the world,
allow ourselves to be tossed
about as flotsam and jetsam
on the sea of life, never to
enjoy the sweet blessing
of spiritual centricity
that can flow out
of revelation
from God.

There is a pulsing
arpeggio entitled 'Faith
to Believe' that ignites our
souls with passion. It is this
catalyzing influence that spurs
our revelatory zeal, but that was
conspicuously missing from the
pedantic charade of righteous
behavior that was embraced
by the Pharisees of old,
and that is absent in
so many circles
even today.

As we rehearse in our minds the expression of our witness that Jesus is our Savior, it is with a zealous rapture that we hear the music of a revelatory symphony that has been scored for every imaginable instrument. We have the faith to believe that God's voice will be heard.

Revelation
nudges us off
our complacency
plateaus, as we steer
away from the trendy
cafés situated along the
broad avenues of Idumea.
We are transported as upon
the wings of eagles beyond the
boundaries of our self-imposed
limitations along a different
highway that leads to
heaven.

As the
circle of our
knowledge expands,
so will the borders of
darkness. The more we
know, the more we need
to learn. It should do no
violence to our faith if we
recognize that a revelatory
understanding of doctrinal
truth might shed light on the
mysteries of the kingdom
that we wish to ponder.

When we
think as adults
and put away childish
things, we sacrifice to a
degree our ability to express
ourselves with spontaneity. When
we stop seeing the world through
the wide-eyed wonder of faith, we
will not only lose our joie de vivre,
or our zest for life, but also our
innocent capacity to receive
revelation from God.

Adults who have
learned to swim with
sharks are characterized
as "seasoned veterans" and
yet the process fails to tenderize
them. Instead, it curses them with a
thick skin containing precious few
sensory nerve endings to leave
room for the revelatory
word of God.

Without discernment
and continuing revelation
to keep us on the strait and
narrow, we strangle ourselves
with material things whose opacity
can obstruct our ability to see how
God has so thoughtfully laid out
before us the smorgasbord of
life, and has invited us to
come and sup with Him,
to freely partake of
its delights.

It is because
of revelation that we are
enabled to envision a magical
place of innocence. We realize
that it is only if we can return
to our psychological, spiritual,
and emotional childhood that
we may rediscover the place
where dreams really do
come true and all of
God's children live
happily ever
after.

Revelation is the personification of God's nurturing influence. Our Heavenly Father is like Mr. Rogers. We see others as neighbors and not strangers. We are less judgmental and are more accepting of our differences. We are less suspicious and are friendlier.

As Moroni taught: "Whoso believeth in Christ, doubting nothing, whatsoever he shall ask the Father in the name of Christ it shall be granted him; and this promise is unto all" who have faith in the power of God to reveal His will. (Mormon 9:21).

When situational ethics guide our behavior, and when every man walketh in his own way, and after the image of his own god, the erosion of faith in God's ability to speak to His Children must necessarily be followed by the chaotic collision of cultural disintegration with the stability of the Gospel.

Do we really think it is
easier to yield to temptation,
and more difficult to resist sin?
Is rebellion simply easier because it
is more difficult to acknowledge and
then act upon the revelations of God?
Is it easier to live in a confusing fog
of conflicting values, and harder to
be guided by what He has written
with His finger on the fleshy
tables of our hearts?

In the Standard Works, we are urged 129 times to learn, but 1,522 times to hear or to listen. It seems clear that Heavenly Father wants our undivided attention. Revelation waits upon our initiative.

Always looking
for the easy way out
condemns us to forever
negotiate the instability of
shaky ground, in opposition to
the solid footing that the Gospel
sod of revelation affords to those
whose actions are consistent with the
obedience of faith. The heavens remain
open and we will never thirst, as long as
our taproots have pushed down through
Gospel topsoil until they have reached
a free, full, flowing fountain of
living water.

We must
have the courage
of faith if we hope to
be able to successfully face
the demons who play a role in
the opposition in all things that has
been built into our experiences. In a
fight or flight scenario, faith can be
the launch pad for the anticipated
adrenalin rush that will carry us
beyond our night terrors to the
sanctuary that can only be
found in the reassurance
of the revelations
of God.

When
we express
ourselves through
positive action that is
dependent on the guidance
of God, the courage of faith
introduces us to exhilarating
emotion and to the feeling of
freedom from incarceration to
sin. We can only have such an
experience by obedience to the
revealed word and will of
a power that is greater
than ourselves.

We may be surprised
to learn how revelation can be
a vivid safety net permitting us to
burst free from the ports of refuge
and the comfort zones to which the
timid apprehensively retreat at the
first sign of danger, to squeak
out their lives as they scurry
about from one shadowy
sanctuary to another,
in a flight from
faith.

While revelation
from God fosters the
development of personality
traits that are in concordance
with the symmetry of heaven, sin
is harmful because it destroys our
ability to nurture the equilibrium
that is a defining characteristic
of those who will inherit life
and light. In the nature of
God, there can be neither
variableness, nor even
the slightest shadow
of turning.

When
we are under
the influence of
the Spirit, we speak
of principles in such a
way that those of faltering
faith are encouraged to take
their first tentative steps toward
commitment, while, simultaneously,
more spiritually mature disciples, as
they realize that present levels of
performance are not acceptable,
are encouraged by the spirit of
revelation to lengthen their
stride, as they walk the
second mile of faith
in God.

It is with a
great deal of empathy that the
Holy Ghost shares our perspective,
but He also sees thru the purifying and
clarifying lens of the heavens. He blesses
our lives in many ways by nurturing our
understanding of the revelatory process.
The veil that has been drawn before our
eyes prevents us, for only a moment,
from seeing all of eternity with
the unobstructed view that He
enjoys every minute of
our day.

When we are
feeling the urge to
push the Lord's agenda,
revelation can be our labor
coach, providing us with just the
right amount of encouragement
we need to successfully deliver
our witness of the Savior without
being overbearing. Many of those
who have lost their faith in the
power of revelatory testimony
have wandered into disbelief
because they have never been
challenged by the question:
'Whose son is this Jesus
of Nazareth?'

Often, it
is only when
we have enrolled
in the graduate school
of hard knocks, and have
pre-paid the required tuition,
that we obtain the credits that
are earned by our obedience to
the promptings of the Spirit that
are the form and the substance of
revelation. When it seems that things
could be no worse, we are at our best,
because we are particularly sensitive
to the comfort that can come thru
the revelatory whisperings of
the Holy Ghost.

Heavenly Father
tenders the currency of
revelation to purchase the
golden tickets for our passage
back Home. We reimburse Him with
soul-sweat, as it works on our sense
of duty, on our conscience, and on our
scruples, to nurture our faith to believe.
We no longer see things as they are and
wonder: 'Why?' Instead, we dream about
things that never were, and ask: 'Why
not?' Revelation decisively helps us
to work thru our problems instead
of working around them.

The Apostle Paul
said of the Athenians,
who did not recognize the
revelation that could have been
an influence in their lives, that they
were inclined to bow down before the
unknown gods whom they worshipped in
ignorance. In our day, as it was in theirs,
when it is our turn to come face to face
with eternity, the experience will most
certainly be revelatory, as we go thru
the mighty transformation of our
mortal clay into a more enduring
substance that leaves no room
for doubt or spiritual
illiteracy.

As we faithfully
persist in the receipt
of revelation, the Spirit will
teach us how to become better
engaged in fashioning defensive
weapons in the armory of thought.
It is with these tools that the Holy
Ghost will show us how to put
together a vast arsenal of
heavenly munitions, such
as faith, hope, and
charity, strength,
peace, and
joy.

Those who are
ignorantly unenlightened
can be argumentative; they
exercise unrighteous dominion,
while the humble invite the Spirit to
guide them in their interpersonal
relationships. They acknowledge
personal revelation from God
as the engine that drives
their behavior.

When we
open our hearts to
receive revelation from
our Father in Heaven, an
atmosphere of collaboration,
conciliation, and cooperation
is encouraged, and we share our
resources with others in order
to find answers to our most
disturbing questions. Thus,
all things work to our
mutual advantage;
we are profited,
thereby.

Some explain
our connection by
revelation with eternity
as déjà vu, from the French,
literally meaning 'already seen,'
in order to emotionally explain
the phenomenon of having a sense
that a current event has already
been experienced. The faithful
identify these emotions as
as religious recognition
from our pre-mortal
existence.

Those who
enjoy the sweet,
sustaining influence
of the spirit of revelation
will experience the power that
stems from love, in contrast to
the Machiavellian influences
of lust and the unrighteous
desire for dominion that
dominate the agenda
of the worldly.

Perfect faith impels us to action. When we follow up on the righteous impressions we receive as revelation from the Spirit, it will be as if we have enjoyed God's perfect faith. We will be endowed with both His knowledge and understanding.

As
Oliver
Wendell Holmes
observed, Revelation
can generate power, for
"a mind once stretched by
a new idea can never return
to its original dimension."
It is the supernal gift of
faith that is catalyzed
by an infusion of the
heavenly element
of revelation.

Revelation from God helps us to have hands that are accustomed to lifting those who need our support, and feet that are quick to carry us to those who have become imprisoned by poor choices or bad habits, or are hobbled by ruinous circumstances.

Our sins
will take us far
from the influence
of the spirit of revelation,
whose purpose it is to guide
us away from the precipice of
destruction, and to lead us to
that secure sanctuary where
the stability of higher
laws abides.

Revelation creates
the conditions wherein
we might be prompted and
strengthened by the Light of
Christ, that we might choose the
harder right; that, in faith, we
might make the most of the
cradle and crucible of
our experience.

The reality
of revelation can
be particularly difficult
for those of little faith, who
throw up defensive dross that
is designed to deflect, disrespect,
disregard, discourage, or disparage
the uncomfortably penetrating
question: 'What think ye
of Christ?'

As
our circle
of knowledge
expands, so will the
borders that separate the
kernels of wisdom that we
have grasped from a yet
undiscovered country
from whose bourne no
traveler will return.
The more we know,
the more we need
the spirit of
revelation.

As we listen
to the revelatory
whisperings of the Spirit,
we activate our capacity
to look past the telestial
temptations of temporal
trivia. We develop a will
or a character trait that
allows us to adjust our
perspective, so that the
achievement of goals
becomes an obsession
of our faith.

Those of us who seek to receive revelation are pure in heart and enjoy intrinsic counter-measures to wicked imaginations. Our behavior is driven by altruism, self-denial, self-discipline, self-restraint, and self-sacrifice. These all come as we listen with our hearts to the promptings of the Spirit that flow to us as a gentle breeze.

Without the softening influence of revelation, we have a tendency to have both hard hearts and stiff-necks. We are overtly and covertly rebellious. We lack the malleability and the pliability of those who humbly seek guidance from above.

Adam and Eve fell that they and their posterity might be able to nurture the moral fiber that we enjoy today as the spirit of revelation. They received the gift of the Holy Ghost, to help them discover the happiness which has been prepared for the Saints of God.

Revelation leaves
us heavy with anticipation,
as we eagerly look forward to
the last act of the Three Act Play,
and to the final pages of the script,
where, having prayed ourselves hot,
we will read ourselves full and let
ourselves go, to live in a magical
kingdom where our dreams
really can come true, and
we will happily ever
after.

The revelation of God points us to doctrine, so that when we encounter the principles of The Plan, we will respond to the truth with actions that have both the form and the substance of a godly walk, and that boldly testify of His power to save us from our sins.

Revelation
will probe us for
pliability, search us
for submissiveness, and
measure us for meekness,
as it hone our humility and
elevates us to higher states of
spiritual energy. It will help us
to be moved to compassion for
those who are struggling with
misfortune, or whose spirits
have been burdened by
the heavy weight of
unresolved
sin.

To avoid the fate of
those who greet revelation
with skepticism, to animate our
faith with energy, and to help us to
remember who we are, we have all been
blessed with the Light of Christ. It exerts a
revelatory influence that has the capacity
to reset our spiritual appestat when it is
out of whack and we find ourselves
indulging, and even binge
eating, in sin.

It may be the
fragmentation of
order that creates the
friction that is required to
fuel the fire of revelation that
warms the world. One could say
that it is opposition that drives us
to receive communication from the
heavens, As we deal with our trials
and temptations, our capacity for
decisive action increases over
time, as it is directed by the
discipline of revelation.

If we
desire the gift
of revelation, we
must "let go and let
God." Only then, will we
catch a religious fever that
spikes the temperature of our
testimonies, and gets our juices
flowing. For the faithful, both
the heavens and the earth are
bathed in celestial fire that
reminds us of the cosmic
background radiation
that lingers from the
cataclysm of
creation.

When we find ourselves hesitantly inching our way through life, revelation invigorates us with renewed energy, and instills within us the craving to redouble our efforts to maintain the integrity of our testimonies. None of us would consciously intend to lose our faith in God's power to freely speak to us. It is only that our conviction just fades away like the slow leak in an automobile tire, rather than as a sudden blowout.

Revelation
has been designed
as a celestial thermostat.
When light from above flows
through its channels, the intensity
of the telestial tempests that regularly
sweep across the landscapes of our
lives is easily mitigated.

Those of weak
character do not
even realize that they
are stumbling right past
the revelations of God. They
are as the blind leading the blind.
They need to tap their way along the
strait and narrow path if they ever hope
to reach the point in their journey through
life where they emerge from darkness into
the light of life and their eyes are finally
opened to experience the mind and the
will of their Heavenly Father.

At its core,
it is revelation
that liberates us to
reach our potential in a
mutually supportive atmosphere
of inter-dependency with the Savior.
He can only bring to pass our immortality
and eternal life if we allow Him to do so, and
if we want to know His will, we must nurture the
development of a lively intercourse between the
heavens and the earth. "Behold, I stand at the
door, and knock. If any man hear my voice,
and open the door, I will come in to him,
and will sup with him, and he with
me." (Revelation 3:20).

We glory
in revelation,
when it expresses
a perspective of the
pattern of heaven that
is traced by the finger of
God upon the fabric of our
telestial tapestry. It has neither
a temporal, nor a spatial, nor
even a spiritual boundary. It
can be experienced at one
and the same time in the
past, the present, and
the future; now
and forever.

The ways of the world can leave us vulnerable to a spiritual sickness that imitates the symptoms of those who have advanced diabetes. When our peripheral circulation has been compromised, we will become numb to the better angels of our nature and we can lose our capacity to feel the power of revelation that flows from God.

Revelation of God
plots our safe passage
through the minefields
of mortality. It documents
potential perils and pitfalls,
charts the recommended route
that leads to refuge, maps out
the success strategies we need
to follow if we wish to live
abundantly, and measures
our progress on the path
to immortality and
eternal life.

Those who have become enamored with their own wit and wisdom wrap themselves up in very small packages. As a result, they will never be able to enjoy the soul expanding epiphany that can be experienced each time that we receive revelation from God.

Faith asks a lot of us, but it also emboldens us with hope, and it blesses us with the fortitude to be able to endure. It motivates us to seek after everything that is lovely, or of good report, or praiseworthy. It does all this by the spirit of revelation.

The spiritual sixth sense with which we are blessed may just be the lowest common denominator in the theory of everything. It is our faith that revelation is the grand unifying principle, and though it is indisputable, it nevertheless challenges explanation on a chalkboard.

Revelation
has an awesome
power to catalyze
our feeling, capture
our emotion, contour
our attitude, crystallize
thought, congeal passion,
compartmentalize action
and convey sentiment,
that lead to spiritual
revitalization.

Faith is impotent when it does not lead to purposeful performance. It is the sizzle without the steak. Real faith involves a vital, personal self-commitment to a practical belief. But in the end, even our belief will ring hollow if it lacks the confirming witness of revelation from the Holy Ghost.

When we
have stockpiled
ample reserves of
revelation from our
Heavenly Father in our
spiritual bank accounts, it
will be as if we had received
pennies from heaven, or the
currency of faith in its
myriad forms.

Our Lord and
Savior taught that
His Gospel consists of
"repentance and baptism
by water, and then cometh
the baptism of fire and the
Holy Ghost,' which through the
spirit of revelation "showeth
all things, and teacheth
the peaceable things
of the kingdom."
(D&C 39:6).

With
revelation,
we are caught
up in a rapture
where we can almost
hear legions of angels
who confirm that the earth
has become "a machine for
the making of gods."
(Henri Bergson).

If we were
permitted to look
with a revelatory eye
thru a spiritual prism,
we would be able to see
beyond the limited horizon
of our sight, all the way into
eternity. Through the power of
the Holy Ghost, our eyes would
be opened to understand the
the things of God.

When we have
been infused with
the revelations of God,
our "bodies shall be filled
with light, and there shall be
no darkness in (us); and that
body which is filled with light
comprehendeth all things."
(D&C 88:67).

Hidden within the
fabric of the principle
of revelation is a golden
ticket that bestows upon each
of us the means to claim the
blessings of heaven if we but
endure to the end in faith,
while we yet dwell on
the earth.

No matter how
wide the net is cast,
science cannot explain
the flickering shadows of
eternity that dance all around
us, as the familiar features of
mortality are illuminated for
all of the children of God
to see, by the brightly
burning lamp of
revelation.

Revelation
from our Father
in Heaven can prepare
us to move onward along
a steady course of progress
without encumbering ourselves
with the wobbly constraints of
uncertainty that always lie in
wait to mislead those who
manifest a timid and
hesitant spiritual
constitution.

It is our
shield of faith
in the revealed word
of God that protects us
from worldly contaminants
of our material prosperity; those
things that manifest themselves as
temptation to fill space with telestial
trinkets that can canker our souls
if they are viewed or used
unwisely.

Revelation
refreshingly purifies
us from caustic influences,
and decontaminates us from
the toxicity that is so prevalent
in the world. It neutralizes the
homogenization process that
occurs when we are tossed
about by the vagaries
of life.

Without
the influence of
revelation, we seek
after signs to fill in the
voids in our lives. When we
are past feeling, we require a
greater and greater intensity
of stimulation to receive the
same level of temporal or
theological gratification.
What we have been
given is never
enough.

It makes
very little difference
to our Father in Heaven
whether we are combating the
influences of the Seven Deadly
Sins, or the garden-variety of
transgressions that we commit
every day. Revelation from
God is always there to
guide us back to the
strait and narrow
way.

Revelation is as
a nursemaid to the
nations. Its ministry
reaches out to lift up
the downtrodden and
those who are poor in
spirit, as well as to
help those who are
firm in the faith
to continue the
struggle.

Joseph's
coat of many colors
is a symbol of our faith
in the revealed word of
God; that every cloud
has a silver lining and
that even the darkest
night is followed by
a promise at the
dawning of a
new day.

Sooner or later,
every member of the
Church will encounter
a line drawn in the sand.
Those who have the faith to
call down revelation from
heaven, and endure to the
end in righteousness, the
same shall be saved.
(Matthew 24:13).

Those who
enjoy the fruits
of faith consecrate
their lives to the Savior
and throw themselves upon
His altar of sacrifice, whose
foundation is buttressed by
a superlative display of
revelatory direction
by our Heavenly
Father.

By using specifically authorized and sanctioned words, that have been received by revelation, we exercise the faith to perform a variety of ordinances ranging from baptisms to the sealing ordinances of the temple.

In matters that relate to revelation from God, it is our attitude that will determine our altitude. We must raise our sights and always look upward, in the direction of our visions and our dreams.

The attention and adoration of the world is a satanic seduction that influences us to turn deaf ears to revelation. When we do so, we leave our coats of many colors hanging unattended in the backs of our closets.

Pennies
from heaven
are a revelatory
dowry from Deity
that is designed to
foster our faith in the
financial stability of His
treasury and facilitate
unwavering fidelity
to the Savior of
the world.

When
we allow
revelation to
nurture our eternal
focus of faith, we will
discard "the poor lenses
of our bodies, to peer thru
the telescope of truth into
the infinite reaches of
immortality." (Helen
Keller).

We experience
revelatory moments
when we encounter truth,
as our sinews begin to resonate
with recognition. Ultimately, as
we hearken to the voice of the
Spirit, we will return to our
Father Who art in heaven,
Who is the Maker and
the Fashioner of
the universe.

Revelation is beyond the reach of detection by even the most sophisticated and accurately calibrated instruments utilized by our terrestrial scientists.

No matter in what direction we face, we can always feel the presence of the Lord, for He will be before our faces. His ministry is revelatory.

When a society that denies revelation from God is weighed in the balances and is found to be wanting, it can all be traced right back to their spiritual bankruptcy that is on an institutional scale.

Those with the
spirit of revelation view
their afflictions, their trials
and their tribulations in a
new light, and determine
to discover how they
can work to their
benefit.

God knows us
well, and He goes
to great lengths to
provide for our welfare,
as we shoot the rapids of
life. It is only the life jacket
of revelation that can help us
to keep our heads above water
as we struggle for air in the
turbulence of telestial
torrents.

Even when we
are fully committed,
revelation will bless us
with repetitive moments of
confirmation, when we can say
that thru its miracle, our hearts
have once again been changed
through faith on the name
of Jesus Christ, and
and we have been
born again.

Our Father's Plan envisions a Utopian society, but it also provides revelation as a practical vehicle to drive us back to the strait and narrow way, if our free will has carried us away from the Rod of Iron.

About The Author

Phil Hudson and his wife Jan have 7 children and over 25 grandchildren. They enjoy spending time with their family at their cabin nestled in the Selkirk Mountains, on the shore of Priest Lake, the crown jewel of North Idaho. Phil had a successful dental practice in Spokane, Washington for 43 years, before retiring in 2015. He has an eclectic mix of hobbies, and enjoys the out of doors. He always finds time, however, to record his thoughts on his laptop, and understands Isaac Asimov's response when he was asked: If you knew that you had only 10 minutes left to live, what would you do?" He answered: "I'd type faster."

Phil received the inspiration to write this book while he and Jan were serving as missionaries for The Church of Jesus Christ of Latter-day Saints, in the Kingdom of Tonga. While there, they celebrated their 50th wedding anniversary.

If we
want to open our
hearts to revelation, we
must begin by our taking
a few confident steps into
the darkness. Only then,
will its spiritual strong
searchlight illuminate
the way that leads
to our journeys'
end.

By The Author

Essays

    Volume One: Spray From The Ocean Of Thought
    Volume Two: Ripples On A Pond
    Volume Three: Serendipitous Meanderings
    Volume Four: Presents Of Mind
    Volume Five: Mental Floss
    Volume Six: Fitness Training For The Mind And Spirit

First Principles and Ordinances Series

    Faith – Our Hearts Are Changed
    Repentance – A Broken Heart and a Contrite Spirit
    Baptism – One Hundred And One Reasons Why We Are Baptized
    The Holy Ghost – That We Might Have His Spirit To Be With Us
    The Sacrament – This Do In Remembrance Of Me

Book of Mormon Commentary

    Volume One: Born In The Wilderness
    Volume Two: Voices From The Dust
    Volume Three: Journey To Cumorah

Doctrine & Covenants Commentary

    Volume One - Sections 1 - 34
    Volume Two - Sections 35 - 57

Minute Musings: Spontaneous Combustions of Thought

    Volume One
    Volume Two
    Volume Three

Calendars:

    In His Own Words: Discovering William Tyndale
    As I Think About The Savior
    Scriptural Symbols

Children's Books

    Muddy, Muddy
    The Thirteen Articles of Faith
    Happy Birthday

Doctrinal Themes

    The House of the Lord

A Thought For Each Day of the Year

    Faith
    Repentance
    Baptism
    The Holy Ghost
    The Sacrament
    The House of the Lord
    The Plan of Salvation
    The Atonement
    Revelation
    The Sabbath
    Life's Greatest Questions

Professional Publications

    Diode Laser Soft Tissue Surgery Volume One
    Diode Laser Soft Tissue Surgery Volume Two
    Diode Laser Soft Tissue Surgery Volume Three

These, and other titles, are available from online retailers.

Is it easier to be immoral, and more difficult to be virtuous? Is it easier to be slothful, and harder to be upright? Is it the easier way out to be swayed by secular humanism, and harder to be faithful to the spirit of revelation?

Quid magis possum dicere?

www.ingramcontent.com/pod-product-compliance
Lightning Source LLC
Chambersburg PA
CBHW082107280426
43661CB00090B/951